TAKE IT TO THE
NEXT LEVEL!

FINDING THE KEYS TO A HIGHER LEVEL OF PERFORMANCE

Rick Rassier
Teamwork/Performance Coach

TABLE OF CONTENTS

Introduction

ARE YOU UP FOR

THE CHALLENGE?

You may have picked this book because of your interest in athletics. Great! The principles and challenges that follow could help you take your life to the next level athletically, academically, professionally and personally. What is the next level for you? Is it something you can possibly accomplish today, tomorrow, in a month or year? I'm not promising that you'll acquire elite status in athletics but I hope to help you reach your full potential. Too many people look back at their lives and wish they had done more. If you're willing to be challenged and ask yourself some tough questions, keep reading.

Athletes can always fill in the blank when I make the following statement: The only time we celebrate in sports is if we "<u>WIN</u>" or think we are the "<u>BEST</u>". They also know motivation will likely diminish if they are not winning or the best. Unfortunately, athletes aren't the only ones who suffer from this viewpoint; it occurs in every dimension of life. What is the good news? There is a better perspective. If you are interested, keep reading.

New Year's resolutions fall by the wayside because so many of us become discouraged when we make long-term goals. When attention is focused on the outcome of those goals instead of the process, we may lose our motivation in the long haul. My desire is to create an understanding of the power and enthusiasm generated from celebrating progress and giving us a sense of sustained purpose. Celebrating progress is like the engine that moves the train. Few athletes look forward to practice and too many go through the motions when they are there. Either we are watching the clock waiting for practice to be over, or we would like to take the clock and throw it out the window! If you would like the clock to slow down so you have more time to work on your skills, keep reading!

Celebrating progress is like the engine that drives the train.

For years, I've studied the physical and mental variables that allow certain athletes to reach their potential and achieve incredible levels of performance. In addition to looking at those positive variables, we'll look at the hidden variables that hold some back without them knowing it. What are those obstacles that pull some athletes into the complacency mode, or even cause them to lose interest in their sport? This book will help you recognize some of the major obstacles that may hold you back. If you are a student athlete, parent, coach, or athletic director looking for answers to these questions, keep reading.

One of my favorite posters hangs in the hallways of many schools. It states, "Some people dream of doing great things while others go out and do them." I hope you have dreams, and I trust that this book will assist and encourage you to be a "doer" as well. Having a "dream" certainly is a factor. Many people dream but never do anything! When you truly learn to celebrate progress, you are more likely to match your efforts with your dreams. What is the result? You start to have "Wow", "No way", "What", and "Whoa" moments and you surprise yourself with what you can do! If you would like that for yourself, or student athletes, *keep reading* because this book is for you.

Take your passion and make it happen!

I am not very successful at movie trivia. The majority of movies I've watched I've forgotten. The movies that I remember are inspirational in nature. I'm sure you have a few movies that come to mind. Even the music in many of those movies sticks with us. These movies are typically about people who have accomplished something: those who have taken their passion, and made it happen. How do you make it happen? In real life, or in the movies, what separates the dreamers from the doers? Motivation is a mystery. However, in the pages that follow, my plan is to unravel segments of the mystery - enough for you to get a solid grip on the motivation piece as it applies to you. I will answer some of the following questions that relate to the mystery:

Do we really understand goal setting?

Are some people just naturally talented or is it more about hard work?

What is the difference between the pursuit of excellence and the pursuit of winning?

What creates the enthusiasm needed to train hard in the off-season? What gets them to take the initiative to do things they know would make them better?

What creates the motivation to do the little things?

Why are the majority of athletes going through the motions in practice?

Is focus a skill that can be developed?

Why do many athletes give up so easily when they get frustrated, encounter setbacks or adversity?

What role does an athlete have in recognizing how to improve their performance?

Is mental toughness something we can develop and control?

Why are some athletes able to sustain the motivation to workout and practice with a purpose even when they may not always feel like it?

What are the keys to developing and sustaining intensity?

What holds you back in any way, shape, or form? Do you recognize your obstacles?

What are some of the key factors in developing confidence?

You'll find the answers to these questions and many more. If the issues presented in this book get you thinking, and then you make positive, productive change in your life, I will have accomplished my goal. Regardless of who you are, there is always another level.   Reading this book will not only change your game, it will change your life.

MEET THE CAST

Throughout the book, you will find a cast of characters. Their stories help bring some of the applications and challenges to life. You may be able to identify with them, their parents or their coaches. Each cast member is fictional because their stories are not complete representations of any one person.

Brad – Brad is a potential all-star athlete with a major attitude. As much as his parents say they want to help him, they seem to have given up after dealing with multiple issues at home and at school. Both of Brad's parents are employed by the school district. The new basketball coach challenges Brad unlike anyone else ever has and it could be just what Brad needs to push him one way or the other.

Gretchen – Gretchen is a small town athlete who has no idea what she or her team is capable of accomplishing. Since neither one of her parents participated in sports when they were younger, they never thought it was a worthwhile endeavor outside of a pick up game with friends. Gretchen is rather intense. She is intimidating to most of her teammates and that isn't what their struggling high school soccer program needs. Is there hope for Gretchen and her teammates? What will she learn about leadership?

Jeff – Jeff is an athlete with average physical abilities but no one works as hard as he does. He has dreams of greatness in baseball, but never even thinks of sharing them with anyone until he meets Debbie. How does she shake things up?

Jill – Everyone knows Jill because she is a standout gymnast from one of the top high school programs in the country. Her dad is seldom around and her mom seems to live her life through Jill's accomplishments. Jill's teammates and classmates think she has it all together, but does she? What happens when the pressure gets to be too much?

Olivia – Olivia is like the other 8th grade girls in class. However, many of her friends are boy crazy and she isn't so sure about the "boy" drama. Her first love is tennis, but she knows her mom could never afford lessons or camps. Does tennis fall by the wayside or does she learn to push for the next level in spite of her circumstances?

PART I

STRIVING

FOR THE NEXT

LEVEL

Chapter 1

PURSUIT OF

EXCELLENCE OR

THE PURSUIT OF

WINNING

How competitive are you? Are you a "win at all costs" type of person or do you not care at all about the outcome of any game? Do you feel like you're on top of the world if you win? What happens to your self-esteem if you lose? Do you feel defeated? Maybe you don't consciously think about these questions. Our society certainly places the emphasis on winning. The number one question asked by parents when kids get home from an athletic event is, "Did you win?" Young athletes pick up powerful messages about what is important from their coaches and parents. They learn quickly what seems to be important. Athletes can miss the excitement connected to the process of taking their abilities to the next level when most or all the emphasis is placed on winning. Therefore, it comes as no surprise that many athletes fail to pay attention to the process and find practice to be boring, or pointless.

Olivia was the type of athlete who felt an incredible sense of defeat when she lost a match, even if she was beat by an older more experienced tennis player. Losing meant failure and failure just wasn't acceptable. Her measure of success was entirely based on the outcome of a match, regardless of how she played. To her, it was all about winning. Unable to point out highs or lows in terms of her performance, Olivia wasn't even in touch with the detailed components of her game. The performance aspect seemed irrelevant to her. She had been unable to see the connection between her level of performance and the outcome of a match. Winning is a great goal, but if it becomes the main thing and the only thing, we tend to lose sight of the process. The fear of losing will get the best of us.

How many times has an obnoxious parent spoiled an athletic event you've attended? They yell from the crowd, taking on either a coaching or an officiating role. Of course, they tend to think they know everything about the game. Their self-esteem seems to be based on the outcome of an athletic game or the performance of their child. One of the ugliest things in sports is parents living their lives through their kids. Some parents are not aware of how their behavior negatively affects their son's or daughter's performance and motivation. When athletes worry about the outcome of an athletic event, they are not able to think and play in the moment. Many athletes/teams defeat themselves when the fear gets the best of them. Whether it is the fear of losing, the fear of making a mistake, or the fear of not meeting someone's expectations, fear becomes a huge inhibitor. When this happens, fear prevents athletes from being able to focus. If an athlete, coach, or parent is more concerned about *winning* the game than *learning* from the game, something is wrong.

Brad had loads of natural athletic ability and was beyond other athletes his own age even though he never worked hard. More than likely he got his ability from his dad (Jim), since his mom (Karen) had never formally competed in anything more than a board game. Brad enjoyed the game of basketball, but didn't seem to be overly concerned about winning or losing, maybe because his dad did it for him. Karen stopped going to games once Brad was in 9th grade because it was too embarrassing for her when Jim got so verbally intense. When Jim came home, it took less than two seconds for Karen to determine who had won the game.

Developing the Right Perspective

Too often in our society people associate losing with failure. A team or athlete can make it to the finals or a championship game, match or race, but if they lose, they feel like a big loser. Winning a silver medal doesn't cut it sometimes. Our society paints such a dismal picture of not winning. I remember t-shirts years ago that said, "Second place is the first loser". The first coaching job I had as a freshman in college was coaching junior high volleyball. On one occasion, I watched my team run out of the gym to the bus extremely EXCITED, while the team that had just beaten us stood there perplexed. Their expression said it all, "We won: what are **they** so excited about?*" My athletes knew I didn't care as much about a win as I did about the execution of the skills and the number of times they were able to produce a pass, set and spike combination. They were thrilled about getting better and learning to control the ball. In practice, they engaged in the process. On the bus ride home, I was convinced that my team did not feel defeated in this situation.

In Gretchen's case, it was hard to tell if her intensity came from a strong desire to win, take her performance and the team's performance to another level, or both. Her work ethic was incredible. No one worked harder than she did and she struggled with her teammate's lack of commitment and willingness to work hard. This was especially evident in practice. Gretchen knew the team was not going to improve when there was no sense of urgency in practice. She was an extremely focused athlete, but her frustration with her soccer teammates always got the best of her. She found it hard to believe her teammates would get upset about losing when they didn't seem to care at all about what they did in practice. Instead of encouraging them, she intimidated them by either yelling or giving them the silent treatment. At one practice she yelled out, "We're not going to win on Thursday night by practicing like this!" Everyone knew she was not happy. Gretchen needed to develop into a positive leader in order to help herself and her team achieve the next level of performance. It's common for athletes to have the desire to win, but not the desire to do what it takes to win.

Due to the popularity of TV/computer fitness programs, our physical education department purchased equipment for a dance unit for all grade levels. When I used the equipment for my PE classes, it was obvious that some students scored higher. Not surprisingly, students begin to compare their scores with others and get discouraged. Comparing yourself with others is a form of self-sabotage and may become a nasty habit! When one of the girls posted an exceptionally high score, everyone was impressed. One of her classmates even said, "Zoe, how did you do that?" Zoe had practiced at home the night before for over an hour. She made the choice to practice and her investment of time showed! If someone learns to pursue excellence and gets excited about getting better, they start to enjoy the process more and practice is no longer boring or pointless.

Take the Five-Minute Challenge

Several years ago at the beginning of a new school year, I started a program for my third graders called the "Five Minute Challenge." The purpose was to teach my students more about celebrating progress. The students were instructed to find something they enjoyed doing and practice at least five minutes a day to see how good they could get. Around March of that year, I received a call from the father of one of my students. He asked what was up with this "Five Minute Challenge?" I explained the challenge briefly and shared my intentions for the students to develop the skill of goal setting. Then I asked why? He said Peter (his son) got off the bus everyday and practiced two to three hours on a series of different activities. He said that it had developed into a problem because they could not get him to stop practicing. I thought it was awesome. I asked him if he would rather have Peter come home and watch TV for hours. He said, "Good point. I suppose we should be excited about this since he doesn't watch TV!" I agreed since I had recently read that the average American spends nine years of their life watching TV. What Peter was able to do was impressive for a third grader. He learned how to spin a basketball on each of his fingers on both hands. He also learned to juggle four balls, to walk across the gym on his hands, and drop into the splits. The best part wasn't what he could do, it was the big smile on his face while doing it. He was so excited about getting better at each of the challenging activities. He wasn't competing against anyone. He wasn't trying to earn or win anything. For Peter, it was all about getting better - pushing, striving, and working for the next level of performance. Focus on consistent improvement and you are more likely to stay enthused.

A volleyball coach once called me mid-season. I had worked with his teams in preseason for several years. He mentioned that their "theme" for the year was the "Pursuit of Excellence." I had emphasized that mindset over the "Pursuit of Winning" during the training session with his athletes. When we strive for excellence, we'll do the little things that will help us take it to the next level. This coach proceeded to give me one of the most encouraging updates I have ever received from a coach. He said the girls had really bought into the theme. His athletes didn't even seem concerned about winning anymore; instead they were more concerned about how they were playing (their level of performance from a skill standpoint). That was the beginning of the story. I hesitate to share the rest of the story since I fear the point may be lost! However, the emphasis on the process was the key in producing the results. His team ended up winning the state championship that year, the next, and the next! When we pursue excellence, we free ourselves to perform at the level we are capable of because the grip of fear doesn't hold us down. Talent obviously wins games, but the pursuit of excellence will develop talent faster than the pursuit of winning and it allows us to play at a higher level without letting fear disable us. I'll visit fear later on as well.

I had some great discussions with a college basketball coach while working out at a fitness center. We spent a fair amount of time debating how coaches influence their athletes' performance, good or bad. He was honest and mentioned how down in the dumps he felt when his team was defeated. I suggested that his players might notice his mood and how it could affect their performance. I tried to explain the difference between the "pursuit of excellence" and the "pursuit of winning" but felt like I was not getting through to him. We came back to this same topic frequently for several weeks until one day a light bulb came on. He shared how he thought the pursuit of excellence seemed to be a cop out, or an excuse. He felt that if you were not in the pursuit of winning frame of mind, you had adopted the "it doesn't matter who wins" attitude and you could not be as competitive as you needed to be. He started to understand how the *pursuit of excellence* actually allows us to be MORE competitive.

Consider some of the statements below regarding the difference between the Pursuit of Excellence and the Pursuit of Winning…

The Pursuit of Winning often leaves us feeling like a loser, while the Pursuit of Excellence produces a winner, regardless of the outcome.

The Pursuit of Winning often wears you out during the course of a season, while the Pursuit of Excellence keeps you up for the mission and taking it to the next level.

The Pursuit of Winning may ZAP your energy, while the Pursuit of Excellence energizes you.

The Pursuit of Winning may eventually burn you out, while the Pursuit of Excellence fires you up.

The Pursuit of Winning looks at the scoreboard to measure success, while the Pursuit of Excellence measures where you have come from, and how much you've improved.

The Pursuit of Winning is outcome oriented. The Pursuit of Excellence is process oriented. Excellence goes way beyond winning and losing.

The Pursuit of Winning creates the fear of losing which easily becomes one of the greatest inhibitors of performance. The Pursuit of Excellence releases athletes from the fear factor and the negative impact fear has on performance.

The Pursuit of Winning may leave you feeling empty if you lose. The Pursuit of Excellence always gives you something.

The Pursuit of Winning may inhibit what you can learn from competition, while the Pursuit of Excellence is the ticket to learning.

The Pursuit of Winning may leave you disappointed. The Pursuit of Excellence never disappoints.

The Pursuit of Winning leaves you hanging your head over mistakes, while the Pursuit of Excellence allows you to learn from the experience.

The Pursuit of Winning most often depends on extrinsic motivation as the main source of fuel, while the Pursuit of Excellence uses the fuel that is produced from within.

The Pursuit of Winning can tear a team apart. The Pursuit of Excellence brings a team together.

The Pursuit of Winning assigns blame (coaches, athletes, officials) when the Pursuit of Excellence celebrates the journey.

The Pursuit of Winning may suck the fun right out of a sport you love. The Pursuit of Excellence takes practice and competitions to another level of fun.

Only when we pursue excellence, do we find out what we are capable of doing. **When we are able to put to rest the confining, restricting and choking powers of the pursuit of winning, our quest for excellence is like no other journey.** When we come to grips with the fact that it isn't so much about being the best, but about challenging our limits and taking our performance to the next level, we really find out what we are capable of accomplishing.

Jill lived for practice because she loved working hard without the pressure of performance. At times she felt it might be easier if she was not one of the top gymnasts in the state because then people wouldn't expect so much out of her, especially her mom. On more than one occasion, Jill over-heard her mom (Cathy) telling others about her "Olympic potential". Jill loved the sense of pride she felt from her mom when she performed well, but at the same time, she couldn't help feel her mom's disappointment when she didn't win. In the past, Jill had pretended to be sick just to avoid a meet. Cathy had no idea how her perspective affected her daughter. Jill and Cathy seemed to be on opposite ends of the spectrum when it came to the pursuit of excellence and the pursuit of winning.

Jeff was average in terms of athletic ability, but had a relentless sense of determination. It didn't matter how long it might take, Jeff would do whatever he needed to get better. His parents could only attend a few games each season because of their work schedule. They were happy Jeff was involved in sports because they figured it would keep him out of trouble. In football and baseball, the teams he played on were all in the "middle of the pack" in terms of wins and losses. Jeff wasn't discouraged, and continued to work hard. As he improved his own performance, his confidence grew. One of his coaches in youth baseball had said, "You have to believe you can do it" and Jeff never forgot it. He was most passionate about baseball. As a sophomore, he received the MIP (Most Improved Player) award. Mindy & Greg, his parents were proud at the sports banquet as they listened to the coach talk about Jeff's work ethic and to their surprise his leadership qualities. The coach mentioned how verbal Jeff was in practice during drills, conditioning and games. Mindy looked at Greg with a 'what happened' expression on her face since both of them knew Jeff didn't say much at home. Jeff took the challenges to heart that were presented at a leadership conference he attended with other athletes from school. He read everything he could get his hands on about leadership and teamwork. The coaching staff recognized his leadership qualities and he received captain responsibilities for the next season. Jeff was encouraged and looked forward to training in the off-season.

It would be awesome if athletes like Jeff were more of the rule, rather than the exception.   Plus, the outcome-based, win-oriented philosophy in our society doesn't just begin or end with athletics.   In the academic arena, we want each student to learn, but parents send powerful messages about what is most important: grades and percentages.   Most parents only get involved in the education process when the report cards come out.   The incentives and punishments given out related to grades are too numerous to mention.   Many students are motivated to earn good grades, but is it learning they are excited about?   Some students learn to not care at all.   Could this be because the system teaches us to only celebrate if we win (get the "A") or are the best, and NOT about the excitement created from learning and improving our knowledge?   How often do we assume a person is in school if they are reading text books or other instructional material? Sometimes in the education process, we try to pump students up with information and knowledge to prepare them for the big tests.   It would be more effective if students were excited about learning (taking it to the next level) and celebrating progress for the rest of their lives.

Chapter 2

GOAL-SETTING

DON'T MISS THE KEY

COMPONENT

      While the information that follows may not be profound or hard to understand, applying it can be very difficult. Developing the skill of goal setting is crucial if we really want to take our performance to the next level. After years of working with hundreds of teams and thousands of athletes it has become more and more apparent that many athletes and teams miss the key components. They know goals are important, but they don't thoroughly develop process goal setting or understand how the "process" allows them to achieve outcome goals that are usually set: win so many games, beat certain teams, score so many points, win conference, state or national championship. They want the results, but fail to think about how to achieve them. Athletes and teams have no problem setting long-term, outcome-oriented goals, but neglect the process of setting short-term, skill-specific, detail-oriented and performance-related goals.

Olivia, for example, was determined to improve because she wanted to win so badly when she played tennis. Not lacking in determination, she spent a lot of time hitting against the garage door at her house despite the fact that the driveway was far from smooth. She wanted to improve her serve and volleys, but those were merely broad range outcome goals because she wasn't breaking the skills down to figure out what she really needed to do to improve those elements of her game. In some respects, Olivia was reinforcing bad habits when she was practicing. If she was able to break down the serve into manageable chunks, she would get more excited about learning the game and be able to practice with a purpose. She didn't have good extension on the serve and wasn't utilizing her whole body and the transfer of weight. When she developed a greater sense for performance goals, she would be on a mission.

I hesitate to *refer* to this segment as goal setting because the words are so familiar -- dangerously so. Why? Quite simply, goal setting is MUCH MORE than what we think! We rarely dig deep enough to sustain motivation. I thought for a long time about trying to attach a new name to the concept of "goal setting" but our perception is what needs to be changed, not the name. Whether in athletics, academics, personal fitness, relationships, or professional aspirations, we comprehend only about 10% of the concept of goal setting: the end result. Because of this perspective, many people don't get much farther than just thinking about it or writing down long term goals. Goal setting is 90% about the "process" and 10% "outcome". Unfortunately, if we miss the process component of goal setting, we miss a great deal of the excitement if we don't learn to *celebrate progress*. We need to learn how to establish motivational momentum that isn't solely related to the outcome of a game! The only time we celebrate in athletics is if we _____ (you know the answer) or think we are the _____! This is tragic!

Jill wanted to be the best gymnast she could be and her desire showed in practice. She was engaged in workouts and got excited every time she performed even the smallest detail better or more consistently. Her coach, Ashley, noticed that Jill's level of excitement for meets was low compared to her frame of mind in practice. For most athletes it was the other way around. Before a meet, Jill broke down and cried as she shared with her coach about the pressure she felt from her mom. Ashley wasn't surprised. She encouraged Jill to keep her practice attitude at meets and be excited about sharing what she knew she could do in competition without worrying about the outcome. Ashley believed Jill was encouraged after having had the chance to talk about the pressure she felt to win from her mom, but knew it wasn't the last time they would talk about it.

*We miss a great deal of the excitement if we don't
learn to celebrate progress!*

After playing volleyball for 32 years, I wanted to try something new. It wasn't that I couldn't improve my volleyball skills but at 50 years old I knew that taking my physical abilities to another level was going to be rather difficult. I wanted to get out of my comfort zone and go through the learning process all over again. I was itching to celebrate progress. Our family had kayaked in traditional kayaks for years on lakes and rivers. I'm not really sure what got me to the Kettle River in Sandstone, Minnesota for a "Whitewater Festival" but when I was introduced to the concept of playboating, also known as freestyle whitewater kayaking, I knew I had found the perfect sport. This style of kayaking is more about finding "play spots" on the big waves and wave holes where you can do tricks and not so much about going down the river. It is an awesome whole body workout. Good playboaters are able to carve on waves like snowboarders, do spins, cartwheels and different types of loops during which the boat comes completely out of the water!

As I'm writing this, it's winter in Minnesota and the lakes and rivers are frozen solid. There is no off-season if you really want to take it to the next level. My alternative is the pool. I'm fortunate to have access to a pool at Foley High School, thirty steps down the hall from my elementary gym. I have a plan for each practice session. I wish I had a coach standing on the side of the pool offering me tips. My mission is to get 1% better every time I get in my kayak. I definitely CELEBRATE that 1%!

There is no off-season if you really want to take it to the next level.

The pool was supposed to be open until 7:30am. One morning at 7:22 the lifeguard put her jacket on, threw her backpack over her shoulder, and stood by the door. I was the only one in the pool at this time and obviously caught the hint. I respected her desire to leave so I got out of the pool, but what I really wanted to say was, "I have eight minutes left!" I was in the process of trying to figure out why I could not cartwheel as well on the left side of my kayak as I could on the right. Yes, I wanted to use EVERY one of those minutes. She was watching the clock but I didn't want my practice time to end. When you have specific goals you're trying to accomplish in practice you become passionate about making the most of every single minute you are there.

My daughter Hope on her horse raising the bar to the next level!

Thinking about those eight minutes I missed out on that morning, I am looking forward to the next pool session. I've always placed value on every minute of practice. The easiest way to tell if an athlete has learned to celebrate progress is by their view of the clock. The clock tells it all! An athlete who wants to take it to the next level does not want practice to end. They would love to take the clock and throw it out the window. The sense of urgency in the practice mode is priceless! An athlete who **hasn't** learned to celebrate progress is watching the clock, waiting for practice to be over. Guess which athlete is having more fun and more likely to achieve a higher level of performance. If you are waiting for practice to be over, you probably won't accomplish anything substantial. If we are going through the motions in practice, we don't feel any real purpose in being there. Purpose gives reason!

The clock tells it all!

Brad never wanted to practice longer. In fact, he couldn't think of any reason he *needed* to practice. In his mind, he was already the best on the team and would jokingly think to himself, "If I skip practice, it will give the rest of the team a chance to catch up with me." The times he did skip practice, it was always an "excused" absence but the coaches knew that wasn't the case and so did Brad's teammates. It was almost as if he took pride in doing as little as possible in practice and being flamboyant about it. He wasn't a captain, but the coaches knew he was leading the team in the wrong direction. It was time to sit down with Brad and give him the ultimatum - "Shape up or ship out".

My desire to write this book intensifies each year as I work with athletic teams. It becomes more and more apparent that few athletes are fired up for practice. Many athletes don't place much value on practice time and fail to see the connection between what happens in practice and how they perform during competition. They aren't as bad as Brad, but somehow, they seem to think that it will magically happen at game time, match time, race time or performance time. One of my greatest passions is to help others feel a sense of urgency in practice and place a higher value on each minute and on every repetition.

Many athletes don't place much value on practice time and fail to see the connection between what happens in practice and how they perform in competition.

When I ask athletes if they are fired up for practice, the response is not just a no, but usually an emphatic "no way" or "are you kidding?" When I ask why not, I get an assortment of answers: "It is boring!" "It is hard!" It's too repetitive!" "It isn't any fun!" On the contrary, if I ask, "What about a game, or match? Is everyone pretty fired up then?" Without any hesitation, they answer, "YES!" When I ask what's the difference between practice and game time, the answers are typically the same. "It means something!" "It's competitive!" "There's a goal!" "People are watching." "It's fun!"

I like to play devil's advocate and stimulate some discussion in response to their comments. "What would happen if you learned to celebrate progress and came to practice on a mission?" "What would happen if you were not going through the motions, but really focused on taking your skills, abilities, and conditioning to the next level?" They normally give the same type of response, "Practice would change." Exactly! And when practice changes, everything improves." You may not have people watching you practice, but it can still be everything the competitive setting is, with the right perspective.

It wasn't hard to figure out why Jeff received the MIP Award. He always came to practice on a mission. In fact, the coaches were challenged to prepare more for practice because of Jeff's drive and determination at practice. One day the head coach was considering canceling baseball practice because of bad weather and lack of after school facilities with all the other spring sports. He mentioned practice might be canceled when Jeff came into his 5th hour study hall and Jeff freaked out. "No Way! Can't we have a later practice when the other teams are done?" Jeff asked. Debbie was in that study hall and heard what Jeff said. When he walked by her table she said, "Why do you want to practice so bad?" His response was like a reflex, "You can't get better at anything unless you practice." Debbie was impressed and wished everyone on the softball team felt the same way. She says, "That is so cool". Jeff added, "My dream is to earn a college scholarship playing baseball." As soon as the words left his mouth, he realized that he had never spoken them aloud.

What coach wouldn't want someone like Jeff on their roster? The pursuit of excellence and celebrating progress in athletics are inseparable. If you develop the "pursuit of excellence" mentality, "celebrating progress" will be a natural outcome. *"Celebrating progress"* is the key and missing link in goal setting. It creates a NECESSARY CONNECTION between what an athlete can do now and what they want to accomplish. Without this link, reaching long-term goals is unlikely since athletes end up going through the motions. You have to make the small steps before taking a big leap otherwise it's like trying to leap the Grand Canyon. Getting excited about the process and learning to celebrate progress is a state of mind, not a moment in time. It isn't a once-in-a-while kind of thing; it becomes a habitual drive to seek improvement. Celebrating progress creates momentum and enthusiasm.

Getting excited about the process and learning to celebrate progress is a state of mind, not a moment in time.

The word motivation stems from the Latin word "movere", which means to move, stir, or agitate. An athlete who has learned to celebrate progress doesn't want to stop practicing because they are so pumped up about taking their skills, abilities, and performance to the next level.

If we don't celebrate progress, we're likely we'll fall prey to complacency whether in high school, college, or professional sports. I love stories about athletes who push for improvement even when they are recognized as one of the best in their sport. Some athletes achieve their "dream" of reaching a long-term goal and forget to keep doing what got them there in the first place. They may acquire an attitude that "they have arrived" and the necessity to get better falls by the wayside. They are missing out and may never find out what they are truly capable of accomplishing. Some athletes with amazing natural physical ability are able to ride the wave from one level to the next with seemingly little effort. The next level always takes more determination, persistence, patience, hard work, etc., but it's always worth it!

"Celebrating progress" is the key and missing link in goal setting.

Wanting to reach long-term outcome goals without paying attention to the process is just wishful thinking like trying to bake without any source of heat or expecting a vehicle to get to some destination without any fuel. Many factors contribute to success, but ultimately goal setting is the skill that links all those factors together.

On a train, each of the boxcars behind the engine represents essential components of athletics, but the engine needs to be engaged and moving. Determination, focus, hard work, commitment, confidence, persistence, and attitude are all valuable traits, but skill and performance based goal setting is the driving force behind all of those traits. Outcome-based goals may pull the train for a short distance, but over the long haul it takes a lot more fuel to keep the train moving forward. Short-term, process-oriented goal setting establishes the momentum necessary to pull all the other boxcars on the flats or over the hills. Goal setting is the master key that opens the doors to higher levels of performance. Process-oriented goals definitely drive the train.

I recall working with a high school volleyball team on goal setting. The athletes were told to write down some skill specific goals related to any aspect of their game. They struggled with this task. I offered some appropriate suggestions for their ability level. Instead of just working on serving and passing, or attacking, I gave them some detailed specific things to focus on related to each of the skills. There's a HUGE difference between an athlete who comes to practice on a mission and one who comes with a blank slate. The athlete on a mission knows exactly what they need work on. They know why they practice, what to practice, and what they could accomplish as an individual, or as a team. The athlete with a blank slate has nothing!

Coaches can play a role in this as well. After the training session, the coach mentioned that she needed to learn to coach with more emphasis on details. If they don't pay attention to detail, their athletes aren't likely to have a mental list either. However, athletes definitely need to become students of their game, and create their own list, even if it is without the help of coaches.

Gretchen did that very thing during her junior season. It was a heart-breaking off-season since they lost their high school coach to a college position. Despite the efforts of the athletic director, no one with any soccer experience was found as a replacement. A first year teacher was hired who had coached tennis and basketball in the past. The off-season brought on other changes for Gretchen. One of her best friends on the team (Ella) had shared how she felt that Gretchen discouraged everyone on the team by the way she treated them. Gretchen vowed to never give anyone the silent treatment again and realized how encouragement would be a better motivator. Although it was hard for her to acknowledge her bossy behavior from the past, she knew she had to seek out each of her teammates and ask for their forgiveness. Her freshman and sophomore year Gretchen wanted nothing to do with being a captain. Her desire to be a leader grew as she began to see how her behavior influenced her teammates. As a result, she was selected captain at the beginning of the season. During a meeting with the three captains, the coach acknowledged that he knew nothing about soccer and needed some help. He was impressed by the amount of information Gretchen contributed and how motivated she was to help her teammates. Gretchen was ecstatic when the new coach gave her sole responsibility for the team's goal-setting plan.

Upon arriving for a team-building session with a high school football team, I found the team had spent nearly an hour working on their goals for the year. As I walked around looking at the posters hanging on the wall I realized that EVERY goal written down on the charts was outcome-oriented. They wanted to win so many games, win the conference, score so many points, hold their opponents to a certain number of points, etc. None of the goals written were skill-specific or performance-oriented. This scenario is common. The head coach walked up to me and asked, "What do you think?" "Well, these are some great outcomes. How are they going to reach these goals?" I responded. He then asked, "What do you mean?" I replied with a few questions:
1. Where is the process?
2. What do they have to do to acquire these outcomes?
3. What does the performance/skill look like?

In order to accomplish the outcome goals, many little things need to be recognized and attained. All the small measurable performance/skill goals are of utmost importance. I spent five years as a personal trainer at a health club before getting my teaching certificate. Helping people achieve their fitness goals was a thrill. I remember a guy in his early 30s coming into the club and paying $410 for a one-year membership. We talked about how he could reach his long-term goals through a series of steps. I was as excited as he was about getting started with his training program when he left that day. Weeks went by, and despite making numerous phone calls, I never saw him again. Why? He had tried on numerous occasions to get himself in shape with no success. I remembered him saying he wanted to get the weight off much faster than I was recommending. He wanted the results, but was likely overwhelmed with the process. He wasn't willing to look at the details related to his life choices and make some adjustments. He was looking for a quick solution and didn't believe he could go through the process.

I stumbled upon a quote by an anonymous writer: *"We must have long-range goals to keep us from being frustrated by short-range failures"*. Unfortunately, many people don't see "mistakes or failure" with the proper perspective. They are part of the process. I thought for a while after reading that quote, and concluded that it is backwards. It ought to read, *we must have short-term goals to keep us from being discouraged or overwhelmed by long-term goals*. You can't get to the top by skipping rungs on the ladder. Developing the skill of goal setting means that you recognize the importance of every rung on the ladder.

We wouldn't try to eat a whole cow in one day, week, or month (especially if you were a vegetarian.) Instead, we have it cut and packaged into steak, hamburgers, roasts, ribs, etc. Furthermore, when we are eating a delicious sirloin steak, we try not to bite off more than we can chew, or we may choke. In some respects, this is what we tend to do when we rely on those long-term goals to sustain our motivation. It would be overwhelming or nauseating to have our sights fixed on finishing the cow. Sustaining our motivation is crucial in the long haul and it comes by breaking things into smaller digestible chunks. Many athletes and teams set end of the season goals in the beginning of the season and it doesn't take long for them to choke on the big pieces. In other words, they get discouraged and begin to lose their motivation. Goals are only beneficial if they change our behavior, attitude, and ultimately, our performance on a **daily** basis.

When an athlete has developed the skill of goal setting, confidence, hard work and focus come together like multiline rope. New England Multiline 3-strand rope is made of polyester yarns wrapped around a polyolefin core. The strength of each strand only increases when intertwined with the others. Amazingly, ¾-inch rope has the tensile strength of 10,500 lbs and works great for a tug of war rope. When an athlete has developed the process component of goal setting their rope (sense of determination) gets stronger each time they celebrate progress. It increases the strength of their commitment of taking their performance to a higher level.

There is a huge difference between the athlete who has developed the skill of goal setting and those who have not. Rate yourself in the first portion after reading the statements below... 10 being the highest.

You're an athlete who has developed the skill of goal setting if you:
                                                                      Score

* Look forward to practice and come on a mission.   _____

* Feel a great sense of passion and purpose in practice.   _____

* Know what you are striving for with skills and have
  a picture in their mind of what it looks like.   _____

* Pay attention to details associated with each skill.   _____

* Want to take the clock and throw it out the window!   _____

* Leave practice with a great sense of accomplishment.   _____

* Have a clear understanding of what it means to be focused
  and fully engaged in what you are doing.   _____

* Train yourself to be focused despite the inevitable
  internal and external distractions.   _____

* Are fired up for the opportunity practice provides.   _____

* Create the habit of intensity and excellence.   _____

* Are more confident in your skills/abilities because
  you know exactly what you did to develop them.   _____

* Take ownership of the development of your abilities.   _____

* Are involved in the learning process: thinking and planning   _____

* View the coaches as helpful and appreciated resource.   _____

* Are confidence because of a positive mind-set and you
  think in terms of what you should do.   _____

* Compare with the statements on the opposite page.

The skill of goal setting may not be developed if you:

* Dread practice and just go through the motions.

* Have no sense of passion or purpose.

* Often times have no idea what the skills may look like.
  Your limits begin where your vision ends.

* Have no idea what those details are with each skill.

* Are watching the clock, waiting for practice to be over!

* Leave practice with a sigh of relief.

* Multi-task and let your mind drift off in practice which becomes a huge inhibitor in skill development.

* Get in rut of waiting for the coach to do all the planning, evaluation, and problem-solving in skill development.

* Would be excited if practice was cancelled!

* Create the habit of "going through the motions."

* Lack the desire to prepare which leaves the outcome to chance. This does not produce a high sense of confidence.

* Rely solely on the coach for your skill development

* Are not cognitively engaged at all!

* View the coach as a pain.

* Are more likely to have issues with negative self-talk and think in terms of what you can't do

Each year I give away thousands of t-shirts at training sessions and school assemblies. I love to leave this message behind on the t-shirts: "Take it to the NEXT LEVEL!" with "Celebrate Progress" on the front and "Get High on Life, not Drugs" and "Set Goals, Not Limits" on the back.

Having established a foundation for the concept of celebrating progress, we can move on to the next chapter about details and adjustments. When we have a keen sense of the multiple steps associated with improved performance, it only gives us more to celebrate. Whether you're an athlete, coach, or parent, keep in mind that it is falsely assumed that most athletes are looking at details and making adjustments already.

When we have a keen sense of the multiple steps associated with improved performance, it only gives us more to celebrate.

Many coaches make this assumption based on their own experience as an athlete. They have been successful in sports and may have been the type of athlete who was engaged in the learning process - looking for details that would make them better. It may be easy to assume everyone would be doing that but nothing could be further from the truth. Still up for the challenge?

Chapter 3

RECOGNIZING

DETAILS & MAKING

ADJUSTMENTS

When I work with athletic teams, I select from more than 150 different challenges. One of those challenges involves 10 bowling pins set 6' apart on one end of the basketball court. Each athlete gets several frisbees to throw the length of the court to knock down pins. They get excited every time a pin falls. Following the activity, they agree that it would have been boring and pointless to throw frisbees with no target - not a whole lot of fun! The idea of the bowling pins is to get the athletes to think about the importance of having a goal, a target, something specific to shoot for when they are practicing.

Some high school teams are satisfied knocking the pins down once. College teams typically want a second chance to see if they can knock the pins down in fewer throws. They often share strategic information with each other before another attempt. They look for specific details that may improve their performance. Listening to them talk about grip, release point, body position and transfer of weight is always fun. Every throw still counts for something. This makes the process more fun and more productive.

How many athletes in practice are theoretically throwing frisbees without a target? No wonder so many view practices as boring and repetitive. When we practice, everything we do needs to count for something. Are we getting anywhere? Setting long-term goals without paying attention to the process is like sitting in a sailboat without any wind!

We already know where Brad stood on making practice count for something. His coach pulled him aside and suggested that he take practice more seriously. Brad responded with a chuckle and said, "Yeah sure Coach." When Brad's attitude appeared to be worse the next day, his coach decided to go with plan "B." He gave Brad two choices; 1) he can take a week off, or 2) be done with the team. Shaking his head, Brad immediately reminded the coach that they had three games the next week and one was against their rivals. The coach stated that he and the rest of the coaching staff was well aware of that, but they wanted to give him time to think about whether or not he was willing to commit to helping lead the team in the right direction. Brad said, "You're not going to win without me there!" His coach wasn't surprised by his response and said, "Brad, we know you want to win and so do we, but right now, your attitude about practice is our biggest obstacle in becoming a better team. We need you working with us, not against us. I would love to see you become a strong leader for our program. It is your decision." Brad was speechless and wanted to argue, but deep down he knew exactly what the coach was talking about and trying to make excuses or justify his attitude would get him nowhere.

Many athletes spend time "goal setting" but the emphasis is placed on outcome-based goals. It may sound harsh, but these goals don't count for anything if they don't influence the level of enthusiasm, focus, and determination on a daily basis. Goals that are broad, can't be measured, or don't specify what needs to be changed to improve performance need to be altered. It is a worthwhile investment of time to establish process goals.

For example, in baseball, Jeff wanted to be a better hitter. He could set an outcome goal, like a batting average. It could motivate him to work some, but he would be much more successful with a plan. He needed to break skills down into digestible pieces. What was it about Jeff's swing that could be changed or adjusted to make him a better hitter? Jeff wasn't going to just 'wish' he was a better hitter, he took the initiative to make himself a better hitter. His coach had already told him that he needed to keep his head still and level. Jeff's research revealed some valuable information.

He found that if he kept a good axis of rotation during his swing, his head wouldn't bounce as much. That improved his vision. What baseball or softball player hasn't heard the old saying, "You can't hit what you can't see." Jeff also realized that he needed to take, "keep your eyes on the ball" to the next level and learn to watch the pitcher. He found an article about reading the pitcher and processing the nuances of the pitcher's throwing motion to anticipate where the ball was going and what type of pitch it would be. He was thrilled and felt equipped to take his hitting to another level.

Unlike Jeff's coach, Olivia's coach never said anything about mechanics or technical aspects of the game. In fact, she wondered how much he really knew about tennis. When Olivia saw a video clip of herself serving, she was embarrassed and motivated at the same time. She didn't look anything like Chelsea (the #1 Varsity player) when she was serving. Chelsea tossed the ball out in front of her and got her whole body into the serve. Olivia's toss was over her head and she could tell she wasn't using much more than her right arm to serve. It didn't take her more than a few minutes to find videos online about the serve and utilizing the power sources: hitting arm, non-hitting arm, body position & transfer of weight, arch, snap and acceleration. Olivia wished she had known all the information before, yet she couldn't wait to work on her timing and apply all she had learned.

In another illustration of details, I remember stopping in on a Junior Olympic volleyball practice. The coach encouraged me to offer tips as the girls worked on their passing (bumping). It wasn't long before my passion for details became apparent. Prior to saying anything about their passing mechanics, I asked them, "When do you know where you should be on the court?" The look on their faces revealed to me that I needed to rephrase the question. I pointed to several spots on the court and said, "If you passed the ball at any of those specific locations on the court, how did you know that you needed to get to that spot on the court?" "By watching the ball?" they asked with some uncertainty. Good answer! Then I said, "When did you know where the ball was going?" "What do you mean?" they asked. "Well, at what point can you tell where the ball is going? How soon can you know?" We spent nearly half an hour working on learning to read where the ball could go, and to react as quickly as possible. Watching the opponent closely can reveal some valuable information in the form of cues and indicators. If you are not 'completely watching' or 'playing' your opponent, you are missing out big time. In many sports, a key to a higher level of performance is learning to 'play' your opponent instead of just 'playing' your sport. When you are paying attention to what your opponent is doing, you can often anticipate what they are going to do, or where the ball is going, etc. This is similar to what Jeff learned about watching the pitcher while batting.

I did actually get around to helping them with their passing mechanics, but before I left, one of the girls said, "I never knew any of the information you covered". My response was, "Well, now that you know, what are you going to do about it?" I loved it when she said, "I'm going to work on it every time we practice!" AWESOME! It was a goose-bump moment! When we realize how much the little details affect our performance, we start looking for more of those details. The more we look, the better we get at finding them. It's exciting when we find them and can create new goals.

In gymnastics, athletes like Jill knew that in order to advance to the next level, they needed to be able to perform specific skills required at that level. In gymnastics, there are 10 levels, junior elite, and then senior elite status (Olympic). Gymnasts are judged on specific details of a skill like toes pointed, head tucked, and knees in, to name a few. Score deductions are based on keeping gymnasts true to form technically and mechanically. It would be to their advantage to utilize the information from the judge's evaluation.

Jill was certainly this type of student athlete, as she knew exactly when she did something 'wrong' in an event and what point value would be deducted from her score. It motivated her to work on details in practice as with her school studies. If Jill wasn't in the gym, she was probably studying. Progress could have been her middle name. This wasn't a bad thing, but for Jill, her biggest opponent in competition or in the classroom was the fear of making a mistake. Coach Ashley was working hard at helping Jill develop a performance-focused mindset because she knew that something easy can become difficult when fear enters in the equation.

In gymnastics, or any sport, the more we understand the details associated with skills in our sport, the more prepared we are to make the right adjustments. This awareness of details leads to a higher level of determination. Determination fills the gap between where we are now and where we could be. When we pay attention to the process and CONTINUALLY make adjustments, we begin to use time more effectively and make the most of practice. As long as we are putting in the time, we may as well get the most out of the time. Too many athletes are going through the motions in practice. They say they want to improve, but don't really take ownership of their own abilities. When athletes take ownership of their own abilities, they start coaching themselves, which in effect is like producing a subculture of coaches.

**As long as we are putting in the time,
we may as well get the most out of the time.**

Gretchen knew having an inexperienced coach only increased the need for each of her teammates to be engaged in the learning process. She was already ecstatic about nearly perfect attendance at the captains' practices before the season. Besides the traditional soccer skills and conditioning, she and the other captain Ella scheduled time with each JV and Varsity player to help them develop practice goals and season goals. In the past, the team wrote goals at the beginning of the season but never looked at them again. Gretchen's plan was to have the players write out new practice goals each week and to help them when needed. Prior to captain's practices, she took the initiative to present her plan for goal setting to the soccer booster club and received funds for the notepads they would use to write down their weekly practice goals. Gretchen and Ella were convinced everything they were doing was making a difference, especially since some of the players suggested they watch one of the local college teams practice.

Parents often only ask about the outcome of an athletic event. Some coaches only celebrate wins, but when we pay attention to details and celebrate progress with athletes, we are teaching a priceless skill. Gretchen already knew that the practice goal plan was creating a higher sense of purpose in training. It had changed the level of determination, focus, intensity, and enthusiasm in practice.

One of my passions has always been to challenge athletes to push for better results in practice. Just imagine what would happen if our effectiveness increased by just 3%, 2% or even 1%. Think of the multiplying return. Plus, having athletes in this frame of mind is like adding assistant coaches to the coaching staff. Athletes who pay attention to details and learn to make adjustments are better leaders. Effective leaders pay attention to details!

**Don't make one of the most common mistakes made in athletics by
trying to obtain long-term goals without understanding the
significance of short-term, skill-specific goals.**

Some sports have whole books devoted to skill-specific details of the game. Have you ever noticed how many books are on the shelf analyzing the golf swing? A golfer who reads every one of those books would get confused with all the information, strategies, and theories on the golf swing and have a difficult time developing a style they're confident with on the golf course.

The degree of difficulty or the level of specificity in any sport depends on where an athlete is with his or her development. An athlete in middle school obviously wouldn't be looking in depth to the same degree as a high school, college, or professional athlete. However, even the best athletes have to remind themselves of the basics and look for the details that will enable them to reach a higher level of performance. There is always another level.

Listed below are some examples of skill-specific details:

Basketball
1. Watching opponents' tendencies when they are dribbling, shooting, and passing. Learn to read, anticipate and react to what they do.
2. Elbow in on your shot
3. Movement skills: pay attention to what your trail leg is doing when you move in any direction.

Flexibility
1. Stretch by tension level and not distance. The skill component of stretching is learning to adjust and readjust the stretch tension.
2. Try to isolate the stretch in the belly of the muscle.
3. Check your breathing. Make sure you are not holding your breath.

Hockey
1. Skating ability (making adjustments in the stride and use of arms)
2. Develop a sense of where everyone is on the ice.
3. Rhythm and timing with passing.

Racquetball
1. Shot selection based on location of opponent. Make the best shot for the circumstance (play your opponent not just racquetball).
2. Let the ball drop and hit shots as low as you can when making contact.
3. Position... move your feet to get into the best position to make shot. Don't wait for the ball to get to you before you get in the best position.

Volleyball
1. Develop the ability to control the ball with the hand – Wrist shots.
2. Keeping ball in the power zone when attacking so you can see the block.
3. Adjusting the platform by dropping inside shoulder when passing.

Most of the goals listed above are skill-based or associated with the technical aspects of performance. Certainly, some could be broken down more, but it is a start. A big part of learning the process component of goal setting is ultimately learning the details that would make us better. It is about learning to break things down. The little things may seem insignificant. Tiny details collectively make a big difference. Athletes who take their abilities to the next level bring a list (mentally or written) of two or three technical things to practice related to each aspect of their game. They know what they need to work on because their wheels are constantly turning.

Athletes who take the steps to develop process-oriented goal setting are more attentive in practice and have a higher level of appreciation for insights and tips given by coaches. The role of coaching becomes much more significant for athletes involved in the learning process. The information and tips from coaches are applied instantly or stored for future use. This ability to recall and apply the necessary information to make adjustments on their own sets them apart from other athletes in practice who are just putting in time. The combination of being coachable and the ability to coach ourselves is a key to taking our performance to a higher level! It produces a synergistic affect ($2 + 2 = 5$). This mind-set is not common among younger athletes, but it is obtainable. When an athlete is engaged in the learning process and coaching themselves, it may be one of the biggest factors in establishing a solid sense of confidence. Preparation is the foundation of confidence. Confidence is a huge by-product of coaching ourselves, and everyone knows confidence in and of itself is priceless!

Learning to celebrate progress brings out the inquisitive nature innate to even young kids. Questions are an essential part of learning. People who excel in anything are constantly asking probing questions. Is there a better way to do this? What can I do differently? How can I get better today than I was yesterday? What may have caused this to happen? What adjustments can I make? When we ask ourselves questions, it enables us to find answers and improve.

Questions are an essential part of learning.

People who excel in anything are constantly asking probing questions.

We live in such a technology fluent and over-stimulated culture that many people have stopped asking themselves questions. Athletes are bombarded by distractions. They check text messages, voice mail, e-mail, or social media as soon as they get to their bag or locker. Then they stuff their earpieces in, turn on their i-Pods, or crank the tunes on the car stereo. There are phone calls to make, movies to see, and texts to send, all while they are studying. There isn't a free moment for down time. The idea of thinking about anything for an extended period has become a foreign concept. With all the driving I do in my work with teams, many times I'll drive for hours without turning on the radio. When we stop thinking, we stop asking ourselves questions. If we are not asking ourselves questions, we are missing learning opportunities. Questions produce answers and in athletics those answers come in the form of details. The learning cycle is relatively simple:

Desire leads to details
Details lead to adjustments
Adjustments lead to results
Results lead to a celebration
Celebrate Progress!

Asking ourselves questions enables us to find answers.

Our middle daughter, Kimmy, has a reputation of sleepwalking. We all laugh that she gets up in the middle of the night, walks into the kitchen, eats some chips, and goes back to her bed. In the morning, she wonders where the crumbs in her bed came from. She has absolutely no memory of what she did. Many athletes are sleepwalking in the practice environment. How important is it to be paying attention in practice? Practice without assessment or feedback is ineffective. We can't make adjustments without some type of assessment. These may come from within (coaching ourselves) or an outside source like a coach, teacher, mentor, or from watching other athletes performing at a higher level. We have to have a plan! The reality of our dreams will never materialize without some structure and planning.

I would love to have a coach standing poolside when I'm working on playboating maneuvers. However, at this point, I rely on watching others on instructional videos online. I'm looking for details that will enable me to make adjustments. When we are focusing on detailed specifics of skills, adjustments are a necessity. The real secret is "searching" for details, cues, and specifics. The process is like mining for gold, sifting through the dirt, scrutinizing, analyzing our performance. Athletes who excel connect indications of failure to specific elements of the skill, in the tiniest ways. Unfortunately, too many athletes, coaches, and parents are overly concerned about outcomes and fail to pay attention to what allows them to achieve the outcomes. If we are more concerned about winning the game than we are about learning the game and having fun, something is wrong. This applies at any level!

If we're more concerned about winning the game than we are about learning the game and having fun, something is wrong.

I believe that coaches who are successful year to year coach details. They spend a great deal of time instructing and offering small, highly specific adjustments. The best coaches are able to get their athletes engaged in that process as well. To develop new skills and take our performance to the highest level at the quickest pace, someone needs to be paying attention to those little things (details) and making adjustments. If it is both the coach and the athletes, the results are amazing.

If you are a high school athlete, make the extra effort to listen to those detailed instructions offered to you from your coaches. Call an area college coach and inquire about watching one of their practice sessions. If you are able to arrangements, bring a notebook along and write down each instructional piece of information offered through the duration of that practice.

If you are a coach, how excited do your athletes see you get when they make improvements? Acknowledge those improvements. If you are a parent, does your son or daughter ever see you get excited about their progress? When was the last time you asked them a question related to their skills?

There is an enormous difference between "doing" the skill and really "working" on the skills. Noticing errors and making corrections and adjustments are vital for improvement. Errors and mistakes are part of the process. You have to fail in order to succeed. It requires some digging, going deeper, instead of just scratching the surface. I recall someone at school sending me a link to a golf game. I'm not one to spend much time playing video games. However, this golf game, just like the real game of golf was addictive. You could play a video game and maintain a rather mindless state, or attack it with the attitude you should approach your sport. A master video gamer displays a different mentality than a recreational player. Each time they play, they're looking for small details that would allow them to achieve a higher score. They 'learn' the game instead of just 'playing' it. It makes a big difference and it is crucial! Athletes should ask themselves if they are learning the game or just playing it. I found myself doing the same thing with the golf game. Before long, I had mastered the front nine with a 'hole-in-one' for each hole, every time I played it. Several other people who were also playing the game could not figure out how I was able to get that score so consistently. After talking to them, I realized they were not dissecting the game. Every stroke needed adjustments and, in order to make the adjustments, it was critical to evaluate and scrutinize the results of every swing. Ask a golfer why they have to go back to the golf course. The addiction to beat a certain score can be intense. However, the key to beating any score is making adjustments and paying attention to details. If they just go back and do the same thing repeatedly, a higher level of performance becomes an elusive thing.

I do an activity called "popcorn" with teams to demonstrate the excitement created from paying attention to detail and making adjustments. The rules are explained and a large container of whiffle balls are thrown out without any planning time. The object is to see how fast they could get the balls back into the container. Balls fly all over the place the first round and it often takes up to two minutes to finish. When I read the time off my stopwatch, it doesn't take long for someone to say, "We can do better than that!" Now they get as long as they need to strategize and prepare and they're excited when they're ready. It is common for them to cut their time in half the second attempt. "We can do better," someone will say again! Teams do it repeatedly, each time making adjustments after paying attention to the details. Usually after three or four rounds of throwing the balls out someone will inevitably ask, "What is the record?" I'll respond, "Does it matter?" They'll say, "Yes!" I ask why? "Because we want to be the best!" Then I'll just say, "Mmmmmm, what if I told you that the time you just posted was the best? Would you do it over?" They'll say, "Yes!" I'll ask why and I love the answer I know is coming. "Because we know we could do it better!" Ok, so it really doesn't matter. There are too many variables to compare teams: number of people, distance from the line to the wall, the number of balls. Eventually, I need to say, "If this is the last time I dump the balls out, what does that do for your motivation?" The most common response is, "Pumps it up!" "We're going to work harder or go faster!" I say, "Sounds Great! However, does that mean that the last four, five or six times I've tossed the balls out you were not going your hardest or your fastest?" "No!" they will say. I'll then ask them, "Well, how can you go harder or faster if you have already been going your hardest or your fastest?" "We're motivated!" they'll say. Most teams end up completing this challenge in less than thirty seconds and celebrate progress each time they get better.

It is hard to believe how excited high school or college athletes get about doing something like this! I was working with the University of Northwestern St. Paul Men's Basketball Team on one occasion and threw the balls out eighteen times. The athletes would not give up. As soon as I mentioned the time, they would say, "AGAIN!" After each attempt, they discussed their strategy and made adjustments. I told the coach that they were going to have a season beyond his expectations! He had already mentioned that it was a rebuilding year for them. They ended up winning the national championship in their division that year. I wasn't surprised at all because of their persistence and determination to find a better way. How persistent and determined are you?

When a team gets pumped up about their performance and decreasing their time picking up the balls, I will often say, "Think about how ridiculous this is. I'm messing up the gym and you are all excited about cleaning it up? (They laugh) Are you ever this excited in practice?" Unfortunately, "NO" is the answer. Then I'll say, "Please, someone say it, we ("sh" ____) be. Every time someone will fill in the blank with we SHOULD be!

Paying attention to details, making adjustments and celebrating progress are the keys to having this type of enthusiasm at practice. Each adjustment is like a mini short-term goal. When you make adjustments and see the impact (measured on the stopwatch), it is exciting. Unfortunately, coaches can't have a stopwatch on every skill, drill and activity in practice, but if you are looking to challenge your limits and take it to the next level, you'll be paying attention to the details. The athletes in this popcorn challenge never ask for the coaches' advice because they are so engaged in the process. Far too many athletes sit back and let coaches do all the thinking, planning, processing, and assessing. Some athletes aren't even very receptive to instruction from coaches. That is a serious RUT and it isn't very much fun or helping the process. It is crucial for an athlete to be able to accept some constructive criticism from the coach without taking it personal. Some coaches "over-coach" and athletes learn not to think for themselves. Most coaches only dream of having athletes who are coachable and able to coach themselves. Are you looking at your performance with binoculars or a microscope? Are you looking for the mistakes, or are you afraid of them? It certainly pays to be actively involved in the process! Don't miss out!

Chapter 4

THE FOCUS FACTOR

For almost 20 years, I traveled around the country doing school assemblies. I had a passion for sharing the drug-free/motivational message. Using volleyball as a platform seemed to be a great way to establish credibility before speaking. The format appealed to everyone because the games were against student athletes and then teachers. Students loved to see their instructors get beat in volleyball. People would often think there was some kind of catch to the one-man volleyball format or just assumed I would be defeated. Some crowds were mild while others were wild. One game stands out in my mind. I was up against a very skilled high school team. Several guys and girls on the team had full-ride Division I scholarships. At one point before the game, I just stood in the corner of the gym and watched them warm up. Very impressive! Two of the guys were thumping the ball down inside the 10' line and up into the rafters. A camera operator from a local news station approached me and said, "I have no idea how you are going to do this". The crowd was fired up. When I took the court on one side of the net with six players on the other, 2,500 kids started chanting, "Over-rated!" Clap, Clap, Clap-clap-clap. "Over-rated!" Clap, Clap, Clap-clap-clap. It went on. I remember flying back home thinking about how loud it was before the game, but once the game started I did not hear a thing. Remember, focus is the ability to fix your mind on the task and eliminate all the distractions. The score of that game was 15-1 (in my favor). For those familiar with scoring in volleyball, this was before rally score was implemented. That game was a classic example of the contrast between the fear factor and the focus factor.

I remember taking snap shots in my head while they warmed up. I can still recall that game in slow motion. When we learn to 'watch' and 'play' the other team, we learn to make the necessary adjustments. The processing, planning, shot selection, watching their tendencies, anticipating their shots, etc. all seemed so vivid and clear. When they served at me, reading them was crucial. I watched for cues. The direction they stepped, the rotation of their shoulders, their arm swing, the hand position, reacting to the contact of the ball, the flight of the ball, etc. Before they even contacted the ball, most of the time I could tell where it was going, unless they were deceptive with their arm swing or had the ability to alter the flight of the ball with just their hand. On contact, I was able to get a good jump on the ball and move in position to pass the ball to myself, then set it up to the net for an attack. With their ability to attack, I knew I was in trouble if they got a good pass and set. One time I went up to block, which I rarely did since they could just tip over the top of my block into the court. I don't think the hitter saw me come up to the net and I blocked him. It was a huge swing in the psychological department! They started making unforced errors and lost the rhythm that is so crucial to the game. The crowd became dead quiet and I watched the other team slip into the panic mode. The difference was the focus factor. Focus produces a reactive sense and the ability to respond to a highly-detailed environment in order to make split-second decisions. Panic on the other hand demobilizes, disables and destroys. There's a huge difference between focus and fear. They are on opposite ends of the spectrum in athletics.

Panic demobilizes, disables, and destroys.

I see focus in two parts: (1) it is the ability to fix your thoughts on the task at hand and (2), it is your ability to eliminate distractions. Focus is "the art" of touching up on the details when you're looking at the whole picture. Just like a skilled painter can see areas that need touching up, an athlete who is focused can see things that other athletes aren't able to see. Focus is the ability to fine-tune the process by utilizing what you see.

When Olivia watched her video clip on serving, she could easily see how she wasn't using her whole body. Her ability to focus improved because she had a clear picture of what she wanted her serve to look like and it created a sense of purpose and direction in practice. In other words, she became more task-oriented. She practiced with a defined purpose. Because of her desire to improve, Olivia graduated from practicing her serves against the garage door to practicing her serve against the brick wall at the elementary school a few blocks from home. It was good timing since her mom had already noticed the change in velocity of her serves and was growing concerned about damage to the garage door. Olivia felt she got so much out of the time against the wall. She was learning how to focus and it was making a big difference.

Do you remember studying the cell membrane in biology? As a semi-permeable barrier, the cell membrane functions to retain key parts of the cell and keep out toxic or unwanted substances. The cell membrane selectively controls the flow of nutrients and biochemical signals into the cell. It only allows things in that are useful and beneficial. This "selective" ability needs to be developed in athletics. However, in order to be selective, we need to become ultra-sensitive about what goes in and out of our mind to be focused in practice.

Gretchen couldn't have been more excited about practice. The practice journals were paying off and the team was definitely moving forward. The year before everyone was talking about things totally unrelated to soccer during practice. The new coach even mentioned he had never seen a team so focused in practice. When they won their first game of the season against a rival they had never beat before, there was reason to celebrate. The celebration, however, wasn't just because of the win. It was an acknowledgement of how much they had improved. The team had begun to see the correlation between how they practiced and how they played. On the bus ride home the girls even discussed areas they could improve and were looking forward to practice the next day. Gretchen figured they could cut the current practice time in half and still get more out of it than the previous year when so many of the team members were going through the motions, instead of being focused on the process.

Eliminating distractions is a component of focus that can't be overlooked; it is like securing a force-field around your thinking. The fiercest opponent of full engagement is multitasking. In practice, mental distractions are the culprit much more than the physical distractions. I challenge you to watch where your mind drifts off to in practice. Focus is your ability to maintain concentration on the process without letting your mind drift and wander. School, problems at home, a movie you just watched, a hot girl or guy in your English class, money issues, bad hair day, car problems, where you're going to eat, or even if you will be able to eat, the list goes on and on. If you're not on guard, you will surely lose your focus.

WARNING: Watch where your mind drifts off to in practice.

It all snuck up on Jeff. He was usually very focused in practice, but his mind began to wander with thoughts about Debbie. Even his coach noticed a difference and asked, "Jeff, are you ok? Looks like you are somewhere else." Jeff said, "Everything is fine, coach," but he knew he was distracted. How could he not be? He had a crush on Debbie since second grade and now he was dating her and was excited about the relationship.

Jeff didn't have a term for it, but he was multitasking. Multitasking simply leads to going through the motions. Athletes who are focused seem to have an internal alarm that goes off when they begin to lose focus or aren't in the zone. It is like wearing a heart monitor when you are doing endurance work that beeps when you aren't within the established training zone.

Ask ten coaches or athletes what focus means and you'll get a variety of responses. Just like with goal setting, I hesitate to even *refer* to this segment as focus because the word is so familiar… dangerously so. Why? Quite simply, focus is MUCH MORE than we think it is! We just scratch the surface and never dig deep enough to have it become a motivational force. I thought for a long time about trying to attach a new name to the concept of "focus" but the name isn't what needs to be changed, it is our perception of it that is significant. Whether in athletics, academics, personal fitness, relationships, or professional aspirations we comprehend less than 10% of the concept of focus. I would estimate that focus is 95% about the "process" and 5% "outcome".

Focus is MUCH MORE than we think it is!

Focus and goal setting are too often viewed with an outcome perspective. This alone creates problems. When so much emphasis is placed on winning an event, focus becomes elusive. If the emphasis on winning increases, the ability to focus seems to decrease. As the emphasis on the process increases, the ability to focus increases and over the long haul so do the chances of winning. You can't pretend to have the right perspective and say, "I just want to play at the highest level," when inside you are consumed with the outcome of an event. The word focus comes up in the competition much more than in practice.

When some coaches say, "Come on, we have to be focused!" what they really mean is, "Come on, we have to win!" This is such a travesty and a diversion from what focus really is. Being overly concerned about winning produces fear. An over-zealous desire to win takes away from our ability to focus. Having a desire to win is perfectly fine, but if it becomes the main and only thing, our ability to focus is jeopardized. The focus factor only increase the odds of winning, but winning is not a means to an end. Winning a game or an event happens as a result of developing and utilizing the focus factor.

I'm thoroughly convinced focus can be developed with practice. There is a big gap between our recognition of the word 'focus' and our understanding of it. Many athletes think they know what focus is, but they really don't! It would be like me saying, "I know (your favorite athlete)." You may reply, "Oh really, when did you meet him/her?" I would have to reply, "Well, no, I haven't actually met them." I may know who they are, but I don't actually "know" them at all.

In order to develop the focus factor, we need to invest some time and energy in practice. We can't allow distracting thoughts to break our concentration. When we catch ourselves losing focus and our thoughts wander, we can pull ourselves back to the task at hand. We need to be engaged in the process in order to maintain our focus. Having a solid understanding of goal setting and developing an eye for the details associated with the process of improved performance is a prerequisite to learning to focus. It is essential to pinpoint components of the process to focus on. If an athlete does not know the specific details that will enhance their performance or what they are striving for in performance, how can they focus? Athletes who achieve a higher level of performance are always thinking, planning, processing, assessing, and evaluating during the process. Their wheels are always turning! They're focused and fully engaged in the process.

Attention Athletes:
**Five minutes of focused practice is better
than two hours of going through the motions.**

The word 'focus' comes up frequently in time outs or at the halftime of a game. Focus would be the desired state of mind in the competitive mode. However, in practice, it is equally important for athletes to focus. If an athlete isn't focused in practice, focus is more likely to be a foreign concept in the competition. Coaches may know this is critical, but many times little is done to change the patterns of thinking and behaviors associated with practice. If I ask coaches if they feel like athletes are going through the motions in practice, I usually get a "YEAH" type of response. We should have a big sign up for practice like the one below. GTTM (Going through the motions) in the practice environment is the result of an enormous deficiency in the development of the focus factor. In order to resolve this nasty dilemma, we need to understand that focus is a process skill, not an outcome skill. We have to pay attention to the details linked with the process if we want to achieve the desired outcome.

We need to see the correlation between goal setting and focus because they are two very interrelated skills. Skill-oriented process goal setting is the foundation of focus, but one cannot exist without the other. Focus is a byproduct of process goal setting, but the focus factor is a necessity in the process component of goal setting. They can't operate independently. These are valuable life skills to develop at any age. Even in the classroom, some get better grades not because they are **smarter**, but because they are able to focus at a higher level.

Athletes tell me they wish they had a better handle on goal setting because they don't feel they are as focused as they should be in practice. Coaches also tell me, "I know we should do something with goal setting, but there doesn't seem to be enough time." However, the coaches who have their athletes keep a skills journal every day always say it is worth every minute because their athletes are actively engaged in the learning process.

Focus as a skill is a concept that is bypassed and overlooked. Some coaches assume that it is something that just happens. After a session with his athletes, a wrestling coach who had been a repeat state champion mentioned he might have been falsely assuming his athletes were in the same state of mind he was when he was in high school and college. Coaches who have had some success in athletics may not even realize the significance that the focus factor played in their own success as an athlete. If you are a coach, don't assume your athletes are looking for details. Goal setting is an information-based skill in which you break components of a skill into workable parts. At any level, it is all about pinpointing the details associated with your performance that would make you better. Focusing on the task is having a concrete, specific, and detailed target in mind. The details you focus on take you to the next level. Having a specific target for improvement during practice and execution allows us to achieve a zoned type of thought process. Without it, the mind starts to wander and practice becomes unproductive.

Athletes certainly notice the coaches' perspectives, and ultimately model their coaches' expectations in practice. If the coach is going through the motions and doesn't get too fired up about practice or doesn't seem to notice details of execution or the improvement that comes from those details, guess what? The athletes will follow the lead. If you're a coach, I can't stress enough the importance of paying close attention to the details that will make your athletes better. Celebrate with them when you see improvement or progress. It is important that they see you excited when they show improvement, not just when and if they win.

Bill, Brad's coach was always paying attention to detail and wanted his players focused in practice. He spent a lot of time watching basketball game film and planning practice accordingly. His desire to make the most of practice was the reason he struggled with Brad's attitude about practice. Bill had been reluctant to take any steps in addressing attitude, partly because he didn't know how Brad's parents would respond. He was encouraged when he met with them after Brad decided he would take a week off. In fact, Jim and Karen both thanked him for taking this action since they had issues at home as well. Bill was most encouraged when Brad asked if he could support the team from the bench during the games. The team had an awesome week of practice and played very well in each of the three games. Everyone was fired up about making progress.

When coaching volleyball, my athletes loved the "goose-bump moments" I had when one of them experienced a break-through in performance. For example, in a spiking line if one of the girls hit a ball harder than she had ever hit it because she kept the ball in front of her for more power I would get goose bumps all over my body! My athletes knew I was excited! This type of encouragement is huge. Don't we all like encouragement? Doesn't it make us want to do more and get better? Building an athlete's confidence plays a big part in "taking it to the next level". The benefit of students involved in athletics, and the way it connects to life outside the athletic sphere, is priceless. If an athlete learns task-oriented focus, it changes everything for life.

Focus is a state of mind that should not need any modifications or alteration when applied to the practice or competitive environment. If you train yourself in practice to be engaged in the process and pay attention to the details, the same should happen in competition. The emphasis in practice and in performance should be about execution. I'm not saying that we need to over analyze our performance. That can be a problem in itself. When you get in that zone, things start to flow. Everything slows down for a focused athlete and he or she is able to compete in a relaxed state of mind. When we F.O.C.U.S. (*Find Our Conscious Uninterrupted State*) we begin to notice things related to performance that other athletes may never detect.

F.O.C.U.S. (Finding Our Conscious Uninterrupted State)

In an ultra-sensitive state of mind, we can see, recognize, and do so much more than we ever imagined. Focus isn't just about being aware of what we are doing, but about what is happening all around us. Many athletes only play half the game. They never develop the focus factor to the point where they anticipate their opponent's actions or recognize how their next move may be contingent on what their opponent is doing. This is more important in some sports than others. I've read stories about professional baseball players sitting in the dugout calling out every pitch the pitcher was going to throw before they pitched and doing so with incredible accuracy. The focus factor allows athletes to play the half of the game unfocused athletes never tap into.

From a coaching standpoint, I'm somewhat embarrassed to share this story. I wanted my athletes to notice what was happening on the other side of the net. I told them that ethically it wasn't the right thing but I wanted to make a point. My plan was to play a game in a tournament without rotating positions. I would make sure the right person served every time so the scorekeeper wouldn't catch on to it, but the same three hitters in the front row wouldn't change through the course of the game. The girls thought for sure we would get busted and the down official would catch it right away or the coach or athletes on the other side of the net would notice. We went the whole game. The girls couldn't believe that no one noticed. I remember one of them saying, "How could they miss that?" It was a TEACHABLE MOMENT to the extreme. That was exactly my point!

Skilled athletes see what is unfolding before their eyes. I was teaching them about reading the other players' tendencies, and anticipating their shots. It became a good reference point for the rest of the season.

In athletics, we tend to have more "WOW" and "No Way" moments as we develop the focus factor. We'll surprise ourselves with what we can do physically and mentally when we are focused. Athletes who focus on the process have a calm, patient demeanor at game time. Focus speaks the same language in practice as it does in a game.

One of the most noteworthy points regarding focus and its proper place in athletics is loudest in the competitive realm. Don't miss this: **Athletes who learn to focus on the process and execution of skills instead of the outcome are less likely to fall prey to the fear factor.** They play in the moment and don't slip into the panic mode like so many athletes do. They are able to remain calm, cool, and collected under pressure. I believe that the majority of athletes compete in the state of fear.

Fear affects athletes in all sports and, in some cases, even prevents them from trying certain sports. Many people avoid whitewater kayaking because they are afraid of being upside down in a kayak. A picture comes to mind of someone trying to roll a kayak. If you have ever witnessed someone learning to roll a kayak, it may have been agonizing just to watch him or her struggle. It is all about technique and timing, not about strength. When sitting in a kayak, the open area that surrounds the paddler is called the cockpit. When a kayaker ventures into rougher waters, they usually put a skirt over the cockpit for a couple reasons: (1) it keeps splashing water from getting into the boat, and (2) it allows the kayaker to roll back upright if tipped upside down. When upside down, if the roll hasn't been mastered, the kayaker ends up pulling off the skirt and swimming to the shore, hoping someone is there to retrieve their equipment.

An experienced kayaker uses an assortment of rolls interchangeably, making it look easy. The most important factor may be his ability to stay calm in spite of the circumstances of his environment (for example, big whitewater/rapids). In the panic mode, things don't work so well! Since breathing is kind of a necessity, the natural instinct when flipped upside down is to panic and fight for a breath. The most common mistake when attempting to roll a kayak is throwing the head up as the person comes out of the water in order to get a breath when he should lead with his shoulders. Although he may be able to get that desperate breath, bringing the head up causes him to go back under, repeatedly. During the roll, it is necessary to maintain focus on the process instead of slipping into a panic when needing a breath. Too many athletes are like the kayaker fighting for their breath in the competitive mode. They slip into the panic mode because of their concern about the outcome (winning) and this is counterproductive when it comes to the focus factor.

As we already know, Jill was struggling with the fear of failure. She had no problem with her performance in practice. She was meticulous about details and stayed in the right frame of mind during execution. Even though no one in the conference had scored higher than Jill on the floor or uneven bars in two years, her coach was still concerned that she wasn't able to nail her routines in the competition like she could in practice. Jill knew exactly what it was. The panic sensation would hit her in the middle of a routine because she was worried about the outcome. The focus she was able to maintain in practice turned into fear in the competitive setting. She didn't want to disappoint her mom. She felt bad for even thinking it, but she was thrilled when she found out her mom would be out of town the weekend of the state gymnastics meet.

I feel it is relatively easy to determine if an athlete is focused or if they are competing in the state of fear by the look on their face. You may be able to tell who is engaged and soaking in useful information and who is playing in the panic mode. The more task-oriented we are, the more focused we are: the more outcome-oriented we are, the more fearful we will be.

I hope this chapter improves your understanding of what focus is and how it applies to athletics. Focus produces the pursuit mentality. Any extreme hunter or angler goes through a great deal of preparation and may invest thousands of dollars in hopes of landing or shooting the big one. Even if you are opposed to hunting or fishing, you can still appreciate their efforts. Focused athletes demonstrate their commitment to their sport through their efforts in and out of practice and in and out of season. Focus produces athletes and teams who are on a mission. How invested are you? How focused are you? What are you pursuing? Are you in the hunt? What is the next level for you and how can you achieve it?

Chapter 5

BUILDING THE PROPER PRACTICE PERSPECTIVE

One of my greatest missions in working with athletic teams is to change their view of practice. Our perspective about practice has a lot to do with our understanding of the process of goal setting. In an activity I do related to goal setting, a team is divided into groups. Each group gets a bag of 35 tennis balls. The challenge is to build a structure five tennis balls high on a piece of carpet. All the tennis balls need to be part of the structure. If they come up with the answer, they get excited! Sometimes they will have all the balls in place, but it falls apart. I'll ask, "What is the most important part of the structure?" Inevitably, they'll say, "The foundation." When one of the groups has the pyramid standing, I'll ask, "If this pyramid (see picture on the next page) represented your season, what would the top ball represent?" The number one answer is, "State Tournament or National Championship."

Everyone wants the top ball. The top ball of the pyramid represents outcome goals, and the other 34 balls represent process goals. Each of those 34 balls represents things that need to be done or achieved to get to the top ball. The base of the pyramid consists of 15 balls that could represent small details of performance skills for each person on the team. One of the most common statements coaches make about their teams is that the team wants to win, but they don't want to work! They want to be champions, but they don't want to train like champions.

In order to get that top ball we have to be playing at a certain level. Teams don't achieve a higher level because they are lucky. Luck is when practice meets opportunity. Luck is the residue of design. Achieving the outcome goals involves creating a design for our abilities in the same way an architect creates blueprints for a home. The investment of focused practice pays off in the end.

A carpenter wouldn't be able to put siding on a house without first framing it. Obviously, there wouldn't be anything to attach the siding to or pound the nails into. In the construction process, timing is everything. We don't want the carpet guy coming to lay the carpet before someone does the sheetrock on the walls. The electrician needs to come before the sheetrock is up. The plumbing and heating should be complete before you put in the dropped ceiling. Get the point? To get the end result (a nice new house) you have to think about the process. Fortunately, for homeowners, we don't have to concern ourselves with the complex series of choices that need to be made in the process of building a house. We can buy an existing house or hire a builder. However, athletes **do need** to take ownership of their own house (skills) and understand the process, or the results they desire will remain out of reach.

Gretchen and the rest of the team were learning first-hand about getting results. Their season was off to a great start. Like any sport, when a team starts winning, fans come out of the woodwork, and the girls loved having more fans at their games. Beyond just a desire to win, they wanted to entertain the crowd. Gretchen was always competitive, and in the past, she hated being blown away by any opponent. However, some of her behaviors from the previous season started to come back when she became more concerned about winning. A couple of the girls had already talked to Ella (Gretchen's friend and co-captain) and told her the team felt Gretchen was too intense in games, which intimidated them. Gretchen was grateful Ella brought it to her attention, since she was worried about it already. Both of them had talked about how they didn't want drama and unresolved conflict to be unnecessary opponents. If they were going to get to the top, they needed to pay attention to detail and recognize any potential obstacles.

We ought to be thinking, "If I really want that, I need to be doing this." If I want a new car, I need to earn a certain amount of money or be able to make the monthly payments. She wanted to earn a spot on the varsity tennis line-up as a freshman the next season, but Olivia knew it wasn't going to happen without a lot of work. As much as she enjoyed being with her classmates she knew none of them were serious about tennis. She had watched varsity practices as she waited for a ride home last season and had noticed they were all business and seemed to have fun at the same time. When it was too cold to be outside hitting against the elementary school, she moved indoors to the field house a few nights during the week and afternoons on weekends. Olivia thought she was doing everything she could do to improve, until she met Marci.

- Ignoring the process -
Forgetting about the 34 balls and just wanting the top ball

- Understanding the process -
Viewing practice as an opportunity to build
the foundation of the pyramid

If we have the right perspective on practice, we won't try to justify, rationalize, or make excuses for why we don't want to practice. Having long-term outcome goals is helpful, but without recognizing and accepting the process, we'll never get the top ball or find out what we are capable of accomplishing. The 34 balls under the top ball represent the needed adjustments to be made in the practice environment. If we aren't in the right frame of mind, our investment of time will not have a good return.

Jeff was the second baseman on the baseball team. He knew he wasn't in the right frame of mind at practice when he caught a line drive and threw the ball to first base trying to double-up the runner when there were already two outs. Debbie was watching them practice and it was on a scrimmage but Jeff was worried about what she thought. He had received a mixed response from her when he told her the coach thought he looked like he wasn't there mentally when he was thinking about her. Sure, what girl wouldn't be flattered? She had told Jeff that what she really loved about him were his focus and determination. She didn't want to be the reason he lost it and wanted the relationship to slow down a little. Jeff knew she was right, but needed to find balance. Debbie was an amazing athlete herself and Jeff hoped they could motivate each other.

The gap between the desire to win and the desire to work for many teams and athletes could be referred to as cognitive dissonance. Dissonance occurs in situations where an individual or team must choose between two incompatible beliefs or actions. In other words, their desires and actions don't match up. I often think about how this relates to practice. This gap between belief and action represents the cognitive dissonance. Changing the acquired perspectives towards practice will help fill the gap and eliminate the cognitive dissonance: however, we need to be aware of how we think and feel about practice.

Everyone on the team was eagerly anticipating Brad's return to the team. He was never upset with the coach for the ultimatum because he knew it was legitimate. The coach even told Brad he could call it a medical leave if he wanted. Brad initially thought he would just tell everyone he had to sit out because of some health issue. Bill knew he was heading in the right direction when Brad told everyone he needed time off for an attitude adjustment. He came back with a point to prove: not just to the coaches and his teammates, but to himself. He had plenty of time to think about how self-centered he had been. They were better without him if he remained the same person. He thought about apologizing, but instead decided to demonstrate his change in attitude through his actions in practice. He was willing to work hard to help the team to the next level.

What is the intensity level in practice for your team? Remember, we don't typically compete any harder than we practice and we don't play any better than what we consistently demonstrate in practice. In an activity designed to challenge participants in the area of intensity, I will suspend a rope about a foot off a padded surface and explain that all team members have to stay connected as they work together to pass over the "electric fence" (5,630 volts) without touching it. After successfully crossing over the rope with little effort, I will get funny looks from the athletes. I ask "Any comments?" They respond, "That was too easy." "What's the point?" Then it is time for my favorite question. "Do you want to take it to the next level?" "Yes!" At this point, the rope is raised to about three feet. This level isn't too difficult but it does take more planning, teamwork, and communication. When the team accomplishes this level, they get excited. After a bit of celebration, they look at me thinking we'll be moving on to a different activity. Of course, I have to ask, "Do you want to take it to the next level?" As I ask that question, I raise the rope to five feet. Someone will ask me, "Are you serious?" When they see the look on my face, it isn't long before someone says, "He's serious!" As soon as they realize I'm serious, they immediately start jumping in with ideas. As the challenge **escalates**, the need for teamwork, motivation, attention to detail, communication, strategy, and leadership has to **elevate**. When they are successful at this level, they can hardly contain their excitement. As they celebrate, I'm moving the rope up over my head with my arm extended! At this point, coaches are giving me some very concerned looks, and the athletes start jumping into another plan until they realize I'm not serious. Obviously, there are safety concerns with this activity. ***Do NOT attempt this activity without the right facilities and a trained and experienced facilitator.*** When the excitement wears down, I'll ask the athletes to describe each level. Boring best describes the first experience (1st level). It's more than obvious that they have the most fun with the highest level (3rd). When I ask, "At which level do you feel most teams practice?" It's a toss up between level one and level two. My point is clear. The third level was the most fun because it was challenging their limits. Team members were thinking, planning, processing, evaluating, strategizing, and working together to achieve that next level. The same thing should be happening in practice, all the time!

Jill was a master at picking apart her performance. Her teammates always thought she was too hard on herself. She figured they wouldn't understand her perspective when most of them were pretty much satisfied with their level. Jill was the only one who stayed after practice. She was grateful for Ashley's willingness to put in the extra time, especially with the state meet approaching within eight days.

Evaluation in practice is an essential piece of learning to celebrate progress. Each practice period is like hide and seek: trying to find skill-related details we need to work on in our sport. These details become the target we are aiming for in our performance. If an athlete in the practice mode is challenging his limits and coaching himself, the next level is inevitable. When it becomes part of every practice session, amazing things happen. One small adjustment can lead to big and more significant improvements.

When I left the health club industry to obtain my teaching license, I studied several different learning theories. The idea of monitoring and adjusting stuck in my mind. It is applicable to teaching and any other area of life, including performance skills in athletics. Athletes may improve by repetition, or they could end up practicing bad habits and poor mechanics without even realizing it. This is unfortunate since they are putting the same amount of time into practice as the more skilled athletes, but are not getting the same return on their investment.

If you had the choice between making $10, $25, or $50 an hour, which one would you choose? It may be unrealistic from an employment standpoint (even though some companies do have performance incentives) but in athletics it is relevant. *If you keep on doing the same thing, you'll keep on getting the same results.* Be careful! Don't let yourself slip into the satisfaction or complacency mode! The trap is so subtle and deceptive it can happen without even realizing it.

Taking it to the next level creates enthusiasm, momentum, and confidence. The confidence piece is so often overlooked in individual skill development. Confidence is a HUGE by-product of learning to celebrate progress. With each step that we celebrate, we make a deposit in our confidence account. Confidence produces higher levels of performance. Higher levels of performance produce more confidence. I love it when my Physical Education students don't want to STOP practicing. They know they're getting better and it is exciting. The more exciting it is, the more they want to practice: the more they practice, the better they get, the better they get, the more exciting it is, etc. Confidence soars as they build their skills.

An Athlete's Quick Tips for Practice:

1. *Come to practice on a mission. What is the next level of performance for you? What are you shooting, striving, and working for in terms of skills and execution?*

2. *Enter the practice setting as if you are walking into a job interview. You want the job! Apply for the job you want on the team every single day.*

3. *Listen, Listen, Listen! Would your coach say you are very attentive and coachable?*

4. *Learn to coach yourself! Become a student of the game.*

5. *Prepare for practice as you would for a game, match, or any other performance. Occasionally you may hear an athlete say they were not prepared for an event. At least it's a start if an athlete would acknowledge that they weren't physically and mentally prepared for practice.*

6. *Take regular focus checks. Watch where your mind drifts off to in practice.*

7. *Feelings can lure you away from your commitment! You may not always "feel" like practicing, but know that your commitment isn't to how you feel but to your goals. Pay more attention to the commitment of what you want to accomplish instead of how you feel.*

8. *Work on the weak areas of skills. Work on your weaknesses until they become strengths. Many athletes avoid the things they are weak at in terms of skills.*

9. *Make an effort to get teammates fired up. One of the best strategies is encouragement.*

10. *Maintain enthusiasm and determination when frustration sets in. Watch and monitor your self-talk! We'll talk more about the power of self-talk in Chapter 11.*

11. *Your attitude will determine your altitude. Show up with a positive attitude regardless of practice conditions or other circumstances.*

12. *Create a habit of intensity and excellence and you won't be disappointed.*

A Parent's Quick Tips for Practice:

1. *Be totally committed to your son or daughter's sport. Despite the investment of time and the expense of athletics, don't ever hang it over their head. Knowing that you are behind them is a huge source of encouragement.*

2. *Be their biggest fan. Show your support during the season and in the off-season.*

3. *Ask about progress. Show interest in their small steps to the next level, not just if they win. Look for improvements in their performance and point them out.*

4. *If possible, be a training partner for conditioning and skills training. They may be embarrassed if you come to practice, but you could still go to the gym and shoot with them, serve some balls at them, take them to the driving range, etc. For example, one morning, while in the pool kayaking, one of the girls from our swim team showed up with her dad. He sat on the diving board with a coffee and watched her practice. I was encouraged by his willingness to support her dreams.*

Coaches' Quick Tips for Practice:

1. *Come to practice with a plan knowing exactly what you want to accomplish. Practice doesn't have to be planned down to the minute, but at least have an outline of how you will use the time.*

2. *Be organized! Your athletes will notice your sense of urgency, or your lack of it. If they can tell you think it is important, they will be more likely to feel the same way. If you are going through the motions, they may do the same.*

3. *Study the game. Look for ways to help your athletes get to the next level. Imagine how your athletes would feel if you took some time and researched a solution for them.*

4. *Become a master at recognizing progress and acknowledging it.*

5. *Be flexible and creative with your practice routine. Never say never!*

6. *Don't allow for shortcuts and half-effort. Your athletes will meet whatever expectations you have of them.*

7. *Build confidence in practice so that it is there when crunch time comes during performance. Be the team's biggest ENCOURAGER!*

8. *Don't allow for put-downs whether it is directed at someone else or themselves! We'll talk about negative self-talk later.*

9. *Use visuals whenever possible. In the next chapter, I talk about the importance of having a clear picture of how you want to perform and how you can't out-perform what you can visualize in your head.*

10. *Recognize and compliment the desired effort, behavior, and level of engagement of your team. Too often we focus on what we don't want to happen. It gets too much of our attention and wears us out.*

I can recall, as a student at St. Cloud State University, walking to Halenbeck Hall with a Mikasa volleyball bag strapped over my shoulder, anxious to practice against the wall by myself on a concrete floor. I remember having a mental list of specific things with each skill I wanted to work on when I got to the gym. During a training session, I would often set my timer for several minutes. Every time the alarm went off, I would switch to another skill, another detail, feeling the excitement that came with progress. I think back about what motivated me through hours of practice and training. It was all about getting better and celebrating progress! The enthusiasm turned into relentless momentum, which made me not want to stop. Every time I trained, I had a plan and practiced with a purpose.

Having the right practice perspective is a key to taking it to the next level and being prepared in the competitive mode. When the time to perform comes, the time for preparation is gone. Many athletes say they're not fired up for practice because there is no competition. Well, in actuality, EVERY practice is a competition with the competition! Weight rooms often have posters up saying, "Your competition got stronger today, what about you?"

I've thought about the number of hours I put into practicing volleyball throughout my 34 years of playing. It was definitely over 20,000 hours. I feel good about establishing a habit of intensity and always looked forward to training and training hard. What about you?" The same concept applies in the practice setting, "Your competition acquired the next level of skill today. What about you?" Think about it. Are you training harder? Are you more focused than your competition when training and practicing?

Chapter 6

LIMITS BEGIN

WHERE YOUR

VISION ENDS

Coaches at higher levels often utilize video playback to evaluate the skills of their athletes. They wouldn't be doing it if it wasn't an effective use of time. The immediate visual feedback allows coaches to point out elements and specific details for correction or to reinforce aspects done correctly. The value of this process is obvious but not all athletic programs can afford this type of equipment. The good news is, however, that this type of replay system can be developed within our own heads. We can learn to become spectators of our own performance. The mini video clips in our heads are a valuable resource. This higher level of assessment gives us a tremendous advantage when it comes to making adjustments that lead to improvements. Assessment allows us to generate solutions to very specific problems. Athletes who excel become extremely proficient at visualization in two ways: playing back their performance and watching others.

It all started for Olivia when she saw a video segment of her serve during a tennis match. She wasn't impressed, and it enticed her to do some research on the serve. She figured her chances of making the varsity line-up would be much better if she developed a strong serve. She was practicing at least three times each week in the off-season and was excited about her progress. However, after she met Marci, she added a couple more pieces to her training regimen. Marci was a regular walker on the track. She would smile at Olivia and give her thumbs up. One night, Marci approached Olivia and the first thing she said was, "When is the last time you watched tennis?" Olivia had to think hard and finally said, "I suppose a couple months ago. Why?" "Because it still helps me know what I want to play like," said Marci. Marci shared with Olivia how she has played tennis for over 30 years, participates in a USTA league and still loves the game. Before she left, Marci challenged Olivia to watch at least ten minutes of tennis video and spend five minutes with a hacky sack every day. Olivia didn't forget Marci's words to her, "You do that and you'll surprise yourself with what you can do."

A common saying (and title of this chapter) is that limits begin where your vision ends. We can't perform at a higher level than we can imagine. We can't play any better than what we can picture in our minds. The benefits of visualization are enormous. Seeing someone else performing at a higher level may be the first step in the process. I enjoy watching younger athletes mimicking their sports idols when they have a ball in their hand. If we could jump inside their heads, they are playing a video clip of that athlete and trying to emulate it. Volleyball was difficult for me to teach at the elementary level until I realized many students had never seen organized volleyball. They had seen jungle ball (a term I use for backyard volleyball) played at a family reunion or at the park. When I implemented more demonstrations and short clips of skilled players, it made a big difference. When they had formulated a visual of what the skills should look like, they were more successful.

Anyone who lives in Minnesota (Land of 10,000 Lakes) should tap into the recreational potential of the beautiful lakes and rivers! I mentioned earlier that I took up freestyle whitewater kayaking in 2010. I've been able to make great strides in my paddling because I watch video just about every day of others doing tricks and maneuvers I was unable to do. Without a clear picture in my mind, I know I would not have advanced nearly as quickly as I have.

Two words go really well together: watch and learn. I'm amazed how many athletes don't watch their sport at a higher level. One of the keys to a higher level of performance would definitely be establishing a clear picture of the next level. Watching just for entertainment doesn't count. I'm talking about watching and learning. What makes someone better than you? What are they doing that you aren't? Are you inspired to practice afterwards?

In 1992, one of my high school volleyball players was selected to Fab 50 Volleyball Monthly (See resources) which is a list recognizing the top 50 high school volleyball players in the country. Some thought it was a fluke since Lori Baynes was from Foley, Minnesota. It was no fluke. Her ball-handling skills and awareness on the court were incredible. She would come to the gym just about every morning to play pepper with me (cranking balls back and forth at each other). Not only did Lori train and practice hard, but she repeatedly watched every indoor and beach volleyball tape that she could get her hands on. This helped her establish a clear picture of how she wanted to play and produced the enthusiasm to sustain a high level of motivation. She took the initiative to do the things that would advance her performance. Too many athletes only think or talk about doing things outside of practice and don't do it!

You ultimately decide what you get from every minute of practice physically and mentally. The athlete skilled in visualization is able to practice without even stepping on the court, field, track, mat, rink, or getting into the pool, etc. I've heard that the mind can't tell the difference between something real or imagined. I practiced volleyball without even going to the gym. When I was at the gym, I would visualize the skills before doing them as well. When practicing hitting at the net, I would hang towels from the net and picture different blocking scenarios in my mind when I attacked the ball. Visualization is an incredible supplemental investment to the physical dimension of practice and definitely worth tapping into.

Both Jeff and Debbie were excited about improving their performance. Debbie loved the intense look of focus on Jeff's face while watching instructional tapes online about reading the pitcher. They had detailed conversations about looking for tendencies, strengths, weaknesses, and habits of the pitcher. The enthusiasm generated from further discussion about the pitcher's stance, grip on the ball, or any preparation that could indicate what type of pitch was coming next was priceless. Of course, there were differences between softball and baseball, but it was helpful and interesting to both of them. One of their favorites was a batting simulator with a video of the pitcher throwing in at them. The time they invested in learning how to read the pitcher and taking swings in their head was actually great batting practice.

One activity I use in training teaches the visualization aspect of goal setting. Teams are divided into groups of 3-5 athletes. Since this challenge usually follows another activity that focused on teamwork, I tell them I want to see how well they can work together. Each group is given a well known 24-piece puzzle. I specifically tell them I want to see how long it takes them to put **all** the puzzles together. When I say "go" it is interesting to watch what transpires. Beforehand I mix up the pieces so none of the puzzles are complete within themselves. It doesn't take them more than a minute to realize they have to help each other out. A few teams completely fall apart. One high school boys' hockey team trashed half the puzzles because they ended up fighting over the pieces instead of working together. Most teams do a great job at looking for what other groups need and are willing to help them out. The puzzle challenge provides applications to teamwork. We are better at thinking about "me" than we are about "we". We are self-centered by nature and teamwork does NOT come naturally to us.

The puzzle also has fantastic applications related to visualization. I like to ask, "How many of you looked at the picture on the puzzle box when you put the puzzle together?" Everyone says yes or raises their hand. When I ask, "Why"? The number one answer is, "It's easier to put together when you know what it looks like!" Think about the implications that response has in terms of visualization. Practice ceases to be boring when you are trying to put the puzzle together. If you have ever put a puzzle together, you know how this relates. Once you find a piece or get a section together, you want to build on it and find another piece. It is hard to quit! "One more piece". Envision the look on someone's face focused on searching for a puzzle piece. They know exactly what they're looking for down to the nitty-gritty details of the piece (shape, size, colors). The process is more exciting when things start coming together.

This is EXACTLY the frame of mind of an athlete who has learned to celebrate progress. They don't want practice to be over. Theoretically, athletes at any level should be putting a puzzle together in practice. The big difference is that some athletes spend two hours and never find one piece to their puzzle. Why? Because they have no idea what they're looking for and no vision of what they want to accomplish. Some of them aren't even looking! How exciting can that be? If we really want to take our abilities to the next level, we have to know what the puzzle looks like.

Planning practice was Gretchen's pride and joy. The coach not only gave her sole responsibility for goal setting throughout the season, he was also open to her ideas for practice. The team had already been to three university games, and Gretchen had probably watched the NCAA Division I Women's Soccer Championship game ten times while doing some cardio training on an elliptical machine. Gretchen had a picture in her mind of how she wanted the team to be able to play and looked for drills that would bring them closer to the desired performance level. When planning the practice agenda, she would consider things like: 1) staying light on the feet to improve reaction time, 2) visual awareness of the field and the position of the players, 3) improving weak side performance, 4) shielding the defender from the ball, and 5) practicing quick touches. Gretchen would someday make a great coach.

Brad was not planning practice like Gretchen was but he was much more engaged in practice. For the first time in high school, Brad looked forward to 3:00 when practice started. He couldn't believe how fast time flew by during the drills and conditioning he had always despised. He and his dad went to several games and watched others on TV. He was becoming a student of the game. In the past, he never thought he could learn much from watching. Without being aware of it, Brad was growing increasingly concerned about how well he and the rest of the team were performing and less concerned about the outcome of the games. Funny thing… they were 12-2 and having an awesome season.

When the time to perform comes, the time for preparation is gone!

Jill was ready to perform at the state gymnastics meet. She was looking at three Division I college programs and two of them had coaches at the meet. Coach Ashley knew Jill was ready physically and mentally. One of the things Jill had worked on was formulating nothing but positive mental videos of her performance. Jill knew that the mind could make more mistakes than the body so she practiced her visualization. Gymnastics always gets high ratings during the Olympics. Most of us have seen gymnasts performing in their mind before their routine even starts. Jill was excited about showing what she could do and she certainly did! She placed 1st on floor, 2nd on the uneven bars, 3rd on beam and won the all-around. She was elated! Because her mom was unable to attend, she called her with the news. The first thing her mom said was, "What happened on the bars?" You can imagine how dejected Jill felt!

Jill thought about how often she had watched the tapes of the Olympics. Besides the time in the gym, on the court, field, course, weight room, etc. athletes also need to watch videos and instructional tapes to achieve higher performance levels. Watch them once, twice, watch them repeatedly. Develop a clear vision of the desired performance. Think about it. Who is going to perform at a higher level, someone with or without a clear vision of the performance level they desire to achieve?

If you weren't convinced of the necessity of developing a vision before you read this chapter, I hope you are now. It doesn't have to be a long time. A few minutes several times a week would be helpful. Find a time where it could become a routine: when you are stretching after a workout, after studying, before crashing for the night. The time you spend watching others perform at a higher level will definitely be worthwhile. Don't miss out!

Chapter 7

FIVE STEPS OF LEARNING IN ATHLETICS

We live in a microwave society, wanting quick and easy results. What we really need is an oven mentality. When baking something in the oven, we need to be patient, because it takes more time. Taking your performance to the next level doesn't happen over night, it is a process and we have to be patient and persistent. Without understanding the process, outcome goals are nothing more than pipe dreams that die and fade like New Year's resolutions. Ultimately, with every aspect of our skills, we go through steps of learning whether we know it or not. When we understand these steps, it equips us with a greater sense of purpose in our effort to take our performance to the next level. The italicized segments offer illustrations from my volleyball experience that may help bring clarity to the five steps of learning.

Five Steps of Learning and Practice Applications

1) Want it, 2) Find it, 3) Practice it, 4) Get it, 5) Master it

1. **Want it.** This may be the most important step of all. If we don't want it or aren't looking for it, we'll miss opportunities to learn.

2. **Find it.** Eventually an athlete will learn about components of a skill they may have been unaware of. It may happen even if they are skipping step one and a coach instructs them on how they could improve. They may not have recognized a particular deficiency in the process of improving his or her performance.

   I wouldn't hesitate to say that more than 90% of volleyball players who attack (spike the ball after the setter sets it up for them) come in too far underneath the ball. This causes several problems. It inhibits the ability to hit the ball when it is in the power zone, and their ability to see the block is jeopardized. Any hitter will tell you that they would love to be able to hit the ball harder and see the opposing block better so they are not blocked. Many hitters are unaware of this element

   Another example shared earlier: Jeff was unaware his head was bouncing so much during his swing at an at-bat in baseball. This was something he didn't know and finding it was a bonus in the process of improving his performance. .

3. **Practice it.** Once we know what area we need work on and recognize particular deficiencies in the process, we need to practice the specific aspects of a skill.

   Once an attacker has the above information revealed to them, they now move into the practice step of learning. They know they are coming in too far under the ball when they are hitting. They want to be able to hit the ball harder, and see the block, but have established some bad habits. It will take practice to make adaptations and adjustments in their approach (the few quick steps an attacker takes before jumping for the spike). It might mean that they take off the floor a few inches further back from the net to make the adjustment and keep the ball in front of them. A few inches can make a big difference.

Remember Jeff: His coaches told him his head was moving too much during his swing and that it had a great deal to do with maintaining a smooth swinging axis. He had some work to do.

4. **Get it.** At this step in the learning process, we can do it, but not consistently and we have to think about the process during execution .

It is all about practice, making adjustments, and analyzing details. When you get it, you know. I remember some of the volleyball athletes in hitting lines who had this as an area of concern. The look on their faces was priceless when they would get the ball in the power zone (slightly in front of them instead of over their heads) and they would hit the ball harder than they ever had. When in this step of the learning process, it may take reminders from coaches to start recognizing when they are in too far under the ball themselves. Athletes may develop a list of verbal cues that help direct them or guide them through the process.

Back to Jeff: Now during batting practice, Jeff knows his head is bouncing. He can feel it and see it on the videos when the coaches play it back for him. However, many of his swings do look and feel good. He is encouraged with the progress, even though it is not happening naturally.

5. **Master it** – It is exciting when we know we have it, and we can do it without thinking about it. In this step of the process, an athlete has practiced the skill so often that it becomes "second nature" and muscle memory takes over.

If the attacker develops a consistent approach, they're able to keep the ball in front. This enables the attacker to hit the ball harder and see the block without even thinking about it. They become more aware of the details surrounding the block. Now they can start paying attention to the position of the blocker's hands, and how to use the block. This may require skills related to controlling the ball with the hand, which is one of the most neglected skills in volleyball. For many, this skill will remain in the second step of learning unless an attacker puts in significant practice time.

Another example: Jeff logged over ten hours of time in the batting cage outside of regular practice in two weeks. Excited about how much better his swing looks and feels he knows his ability to see the ball has improved substantially. The coaches also observe that he is making much better contact with the ball and more consistently. Hard work pays off.

Understanding this information about the steps is helpful. It's all about discovering what we don't know and doing something about it! Most of us have a reservoir of information backed up like water behind a dam. When we develop a thirst for the information, we start making progress. That is why step one and wanting to find the information is so important. The inquisitive nature exposes useful information, which starts the learning process. A key in taking it to the next level is utilizing the information. It is important to have our radar up (minds constantly searching) for any detail that may be a factor in learning.

If you don't have your radar up it is hard to see the value in practice. Brad always felt mistakes and weaknesses were equivalent to failure. Since he became a student of the game, his perspective regarding practice changed drastically. He saw mistakes as part of the process and was excited to find out what he needed to work on. His 'time-out' from the team was the best thing that ever happened to him as an athlete. Things changed significantly at home as well. Karen had shared with the coach how Brad was helping more with simple tasks at home and had begun playing basketball with his little sister.

Jill hung up the phone abruptly without a word. There was silence on the phone for a moment before the call ended. Cathy tried calling back a couple times, but assumed Jill was still at the gymnastics meet and was unable to answer. Thinking the call just dropped it never occurred to her that her daughter may have hung up on her. Jill sat and stared at her ringing phone, unable to get herself to answer. She had just taken 1st on floor, 2nd on bars, 3rd on the beam and won all-around at the state meet, and all her mom said was, "What happened on the bars?" There was no, "Wow, that is so exciting!" or "Congratulations" just, "What happened on the bars?" It appeared to be the classic case of the difference between the pursuit of excellence and the pursuit of winning. Jill felt she could never do well enough. Ashley walked up to her and initially thought Jill was crying tears of joy but realized she had called her mom. Ashley told Jill how proud she was of everything she had accomplished. Jill's determination and persistence to figure out how to perform her best had taken her to the top, but somehow she felt that she had failed. She had learned so much, but still felt she fell short. Was it because her mom seemed so concerned about winning?

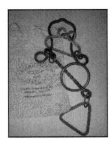

In many respects, athletics is much like a puzzle. We should always be engaged in trying to figure out the puzzle of how to perform at a higher level. To help athletes develop the ability to improve their performance, I have them work together on "Tavern Puzzles." (See resources) The challenge is to figure out how to remove a ring from the steel structure. The Tavern Puzzle Collection is divided into eight groups. Group 1 is the simplest. The groups become progressively more difficult, with the most complex being Group 8. This is one of my favorite challenges for

for athletes. Every minute or two I ask, "Give up?" "NO!" is the reply. Most groups would go much longer, but after about seven minutes, I'll ask if they want one, two, or three more minutes. They always want three minutes and usually ask for more. Rarely does anyone find the answer in the time given and if they do, they have to be able to do it again to prove it wasn't just luck. They always want the answer. I ask them to guess how long it took me to get the ring off. They are often surprised to hear it took me 13 hours. "13 hours straight?" they'll ask. "No, I ride an exercise bike at least an hour every day and for thirteen days I worked on this puzzle." When I ask them if they think thirteen hours is a long time, they say "yes" for sure. Then, I pose a series of questions that define the purpose of the challenge itself:

How many hours have you invested into (your sport) during your life?

Are you still trying to figure out how to perform at a higher level?

Are you engaged in the process before, during, and after practice?

Are your wheels always turning? Do you want it? (Step No. 1)

Are you looking for details that will enable you to get better?

Do you typically want that "extra" two, three or four minutes to solve the performance puzzle?

If you answered "Yes" to the last five questions, that is good news. You are exactly where you need to be! After I reveal the answer, some teams ask if they can try it again after they have seen it done. Every time I've let them, no one has been able to take off the ring. What if I showed them twice? Would it increase the chances of them being able to do it? What if they saw it three, or four times, would it increase their chances even more? Of course! In other words, *the clearer the picture of what we want to be able to do, the more likely we will be able to do it!* This only reinforces what we discussed in the last chapter about having a vision of how we want to perform.

Olivia had already brought several components of the game to the next level (through the steps of learning). She wasn't aware of the steps, but she knew she was getting better. It had been three weeks since she had seen Marci, who right away noticed the improvement. Marci said, "Somebody's been watching tennis." Olivia just smiled. "Did you buy a hacky sack?" Olivia's face lit up, "I'm up to 23 with my right foot and 12 with my left!" Marci responded, "Awesome. Are you up for some tennis? I brought my racquet." Olivia was thrilled to play tennis with Marci.

Olivia had accepted both of Marci's challenges. One Saturday morning she watched tennis clips for 3 ½ hours and it felt like minutes. During the last season, she was always worried about the outcome of the match. At times, she had wondered why she had pursued an individual sport because she had to take sole responsibility for a loss. If she was playing a team sport, then she could at least blame her teammates for the outcome if they lost. However, her new commitment to develop her game had caused a change in heart. Now, she was excited to be entirely responsible for the outcome of a match. She would reap the benefits of every ounce of energy that went into preparation for her matches and taking her performance to another level.

If an athlete struggles to list skill-specific, detail-oriented skills related to their game, they are less likely to be progressing though the steps of learning. The athletes who have no trouble listing detailed cues and information are usually the most talented. Why are they the most talented? What is their mission? They expose their weaknesses and discover ways to become more and more proficient and consistent. You don't have to keep a written account of every detail, but it is crucial to recognize and acknowledge progress throughout each step. Remember where you were, where you are and where you're headed. Remember, one of the keys to taking your abilities to another level is learning to celebrate progress.

I started freestyle kayaking in 2010 because I wanted to go through the learning process with a sport I had never participated in. This experience has provided me with some great insight about the steps of learning as I go through them myself. Even if the water is low or frozen in Minnesota, I still have an informal list of maneuvers on the water that fit the steps of learning I can work on in a lake or pool. Over the last year, it has been exciting to acquire the skills necessary to be able to do a flat-water loop. The flat-water loop isn't an easy trick for a freestyle kayaker because of the requirements: double pump, bow stall, balanced pump, and lots of timing. Honestly, there were times when I wondered if I was going to be able to do it, but I kept watching video and looking for things I could change. The flat-water loop is pictured below in a progressive sequence of photos. In pictures 4, 5, and 6, I became aware of the fact that I wasn't pushing down with my feet (on the way over). When I made some adjustments, it changed the outcome.

It has been fun to bring this trick to step five (as outlined earlier) where I can do it without having to think about the mechanics and timing of the trick as I'm doing it. Accomplishing that milestone has opened the door to higher-level tricks like the Phonics Monkey, Space Godzilla, and the Mcnasty. Each of those tricks involves some type of rotation, pirouette, and better timing. I'm up for the challenge.

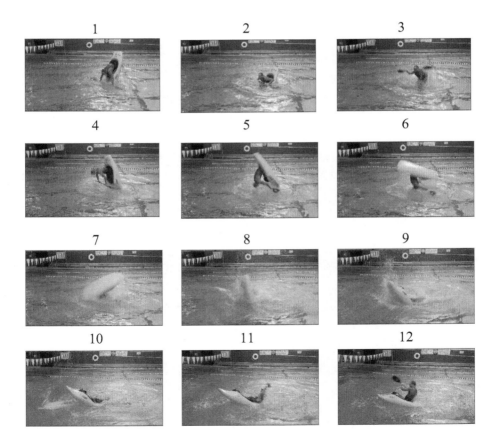

Some athletes move back and forth between the first few steps of learning. 'In one ear and out the other' might be a way of describing this unfortunate circumstance. Many coaches feel like they are repeating themselves. If you are an athlete, how seriously do you take the tips and insights that your coaches give to you?

The rewards for paying attention to details and going through the steps of learning are exciting. The timing necessary to develop skills requires trial and error. When we understand the learning process, practice will not be boring or repetitive. In the goal-enriched environment, the next level is inevitable and we may surprise ourselves with what we can do.

Everyone was surprised by what the soccer team had accomplished during the regular season except for Gretchen. They had the No. 1 seed in their section going into post-season play. Gretchen knew how good they could be if everyone was mentally and physically prepared. Her biggest concern was feeling some of her teammates were satisfied with what the team had already accomplished and had drifted off into the complacency mode. Gretchen decided to write a letter to the team. She knew she would mess it up if she tried to give a pep talk. With Ella's ok, Gretchen read the letter to her teammates, acknowledging all their hard work and encouraging them to keep pushing to get better.

After playing volleyball teams by myself, I would replay segments of a game in my head. I remembered very small details. If the other team was serving at me from one side of the net, I stood in the middle of the court on the other side to receive the serve. I watched the direction they stepped, the rotation of their shoulders, their arm coming through, and the position of their hand. I could often tell where the ball was going before they contacted it. When I got to the ball and passed it up in front of me, I was able to watch how they were setting up their defense and block formation at the net. The information received from that observation influenced where I would go with the ball for the spike or tip. When setting the ball up to the net for a spike, I needed to consider many things; the position of the block, the position of the blocker's hands, the position of the defense behind the block, and whether or not they appeared to be leaning back or committing too early to a spot on the court. This all played a part in what I did with the ball. This was an instinctive reaction developed in practice. All the skills of ball control, reading the other players, reacting, noticing tendencies, went through the steps of learning. If I had tried to THINK about doing that, it would have become too complicated and would have inhibited my performance. There was nothing better than playing in the zone and feeling like the whole game slowed down. When we are in that focused frame of mind, the game flows and it is amazing how much we can see that will bring our performance to another level!

In the competitive mode things have to flow from what has already been developed in practice with a confident mind set. Thinking too much affects performance. Great athletes are able to control this because they do so in practice all the time. They may break things down in practice to refine or work on a small component of a skill, but in practice they also put themselves in the competitive state where they perform the skills without having to think about it. Great athletes understand the fine line that often exists between the preparation/practice mind set and the competitive mind set.

A golfer or tennis player who thinks too much about mechanics when swinging and a basketball player who thinks too much about his shot in the competitive realm will struggle for sure. Something very easy can become very difficult when we think too much. It is a skill in itself to be able to manage your thought process in practice and in competition. In the competitive mode, you want to be able to show what you are capable of doing without over-analyzing every move. It is all about preparation.

On our challenge course, we had one high element called the "Catwalk." On the catwalk, a participant would climb up the tree 23' and step out onto the 25' horizontal log suspended from one tree to the next. If we were to walk across that log on the ground, we wouldn't even think about the mechanics of walking. However, when up in the air, we suddenly become overly concerned about each step and it disrupts our flow. After numerous practice runs on the catwalk you may get to the point where you don't even think about what you need to do - you just do it. One of the keys to performance under pressure is preparation. This moves skills into the fifth step of learning and develops unwavering confidence.

One of my desires in writing this book is to help people discover the confidence that comes from preparation and the joys of celebrating progress - getting people excited about learning! Wanting it, finding it, practicing it, getting it, and mastering it. In sports, as in life, the more we learn, the more we find there is to learn. When this happens, doors open to a completely new level of performance.

Chapter 8

WHICH ZONE

ARE YOU IN?

If you have been around athletics for a while it is likely you have heard athletes talking about "being in the zone." The phrase typically refers to a frame of time where everything is clicking for you. In this chapter, we'll visit four different zones. The zones may help you develop a better understanding of the five steps of learning discussed in the last chapter. Everyone is in one of the zones described in the diagram (next page). You could conceivably be in more than one zone at the same time in different areas of your life.

If you're an athlete, it is crucial to know which zone you are in at any point in time. If you are a coach, consider how your approach to coaching, along with your lifestyle, may influence which zone your athletes are in. If you are a parent, it may be helpful to recognize some of the characteristics of each of the zones in order to take supportive action steps with your son or daughter. These four zones are not labels to be given to anyone. Labels can be inaccurate and become self-fulfilling prophecies. Think of the zone as temporary positions.

The Dead Zone:

The name speaks for itself. Think about the Dead Sea. At 1385' below sea level, the Dead Sea is lifeless. This large body of water (8.6 times saltier than the ocean) is 42 miles long, 11 miles wide, and has 84 miles of shoreline. The salty water prevents any kind of marine life from existing. Its uniqueness has attracted visitors for hundreds of years. If you have trouble floating, you wouldn't have any problem in the Dead Sea. That may be interesting, but when it comes to athletes, existing in the dead zone is downright "nasty".

Athletes in the "Dead Zone" are often uncoachable and unteachable, but they're not unreachable. They may *appear* to be a hopeless case, but they are *definitely not* hopeless. The word motivation hardly exists in their vocabulary, but it is hidden somewhere within. Everyone is capable of being motivated. Finding out what has inhibited motivation or what may restore it is the trick. Being in the dead zone is not necessarily an indication of potential or ability. In fact, many gifted and talented students end up in the dead zone. The gap between what they could do and what they are able to do is enormous. They are like a machine with the plug pulled. In a society that places such high value on performance, those in this zone are bombarded with messages of inferiority, and this in itself becomes a vicious cycle.

A very small percentage of athletes are in the dead zone. Younger students may be in a sport and have no idea why. Parents may be making them participate; they may be trying to avoid going home after school; or they may be there because they have friends in the same sport. They may exhibit the "I don't care" attitude, or even say it aloud. They may have developed an attitude due to conflict with the coach or teammates. This type of athlete could be a nightmare for a coach since they may put more effort into pulling others down than anything else. Give them the opposite of what they expect. Encouragement! The absence of encouragement is discouragement. In fact, if you are a coach or a parent, or both, one great rule to follow is when in doubt, be an encourager.

The Comfort Zone:

The comfort zone may be the scariest of all since many in the comfort zone do not know they are there, or would not admit it. I think it would be agonizing to reside in the comfort zone. Many athletes are content in the comfort zone because it is easier. They don't have to work. Their normal routine doesn't allow them to see the possibilities of what they could do. They might have dreams, but those dreams are always for tomorrow. Tomorrow never comes. In fact, they live for today without even thinking about tomorrow. It is difficult to be worried about tomorrow if you are not concerned about today. Engaged preparation for an event is a foreign concept for those in the comfort zone because they are satisfied with their performance. They may not verbally acknowledge this, but by their actions their position is clear.

Olivia had received the same phone call every Saturday morning at about 11:00 since the end of the tennis season. Bridget wanted to chill and watch movies all afternoon, but Olivia didn't want to miss the open court time, especially since Marci came on Saturdays to play. In the past, Bridget and Olivia met quite often on Saturdays at Bridget's place. Her parents both worked so they could crank tunes and make up dance moves without embarrassing themselves in front of anyone. Things changed and so did Bridget whose only goal was to do nothing. When Olivia turned her down, Bridget was upset and said, "What is wrong with you? You're taking tennis too seriously!" Olivia said, "I'm sorry. Why don't you come with me?" After she hung up, she felt empowered and thrilled to be so committed to tennis even though she realized that not everyone would understand. Olivia felt like she was making significant progress in her tennis game and wasn't going to let anyone or anything slow her down.

The comfort zone is scary because satisfaction becomes a practice motto - often without even knowing it. I don't believe it is always a conscious choice to be in the comfort zone, but it becomes routine to have a complacent mindset. People in the comfort zone will verbally express the desire to take their skills to the next level, but not engage in the process. They could make some strides and improvements in their skills and conditioning, but nothing to the degree of an athlete who enters into the challenge zone.

It is easy to get trapped in the comfort zone because others are stuck there and it seems like the place to be. "If no one is working really hard in practice, why should I?" "If no one else is training in the off season, why would I?" If the athlete is not careful, these thoughts will lead to subconscious justification for being in the comfort zone. The result will be to limit our challenges instead of challenging our limits. A friend once told me she wished she would have known she could have trained harder for her sport, but no one else was doing it, so the possibilities never even crossed her mind. If you are an athlete, be a leader on your team and in your school. Set an example even if no one else is. Train hard in the off-season and during the season.

Who would have thought Brad would be the type of upper classman to challenge one of the younger guys to be more focused in practice. It might have been because Doug reminded Brad of himself before his conversion (going from the comfort zone into the challenge zone). On their way to the gym, Brad told Doug how much potential he had as a basketball player. Doug didn't say thanks, he just replied, "I know." Brad chuckled to himself because he knew that's exactly what he would have said in the past. Brad responded, "Well, don't make the same mistake I made when I was your age and limit yourself by thinking you've already arrived."

Getting someone out of the comfort zone isn't easy, but Brad's response isn't something Doug will forget very easily. Many athletes are not aware of their position in the comfort zone. Athletes leave the comfort zone because they want to be challenged. They know life is more exciting when they challenge themselves. Even if you are the most talented athlete on the team - be careful. Contentment keeps many athletes out of the challenge zone. Feeling overwhelmed or becoming discouraged does as well. Encouragement can go a long way in getting someone out of the comfort zone. It is extremely important to recognize the obstacles that prevent athletes from entering the challenge zone. Understanding what can keep you out of the challenge zone or knock you out is crucial. It is like a tug of war between determination and complacency. The stronger one wins. Having a plan of attack is a necessity.

Challenge Zone:

The choice to enter the "Challenge Zone" may be one of the best choices of your life. It's like a going from 'limiting our challenges' to 'challenging our limits'. In the comfort zone we limit our challenges, and in the challenge zone we challenge our limits! The comparison may seem simplistic, yet it is an accurate way to describe the difference between the athletes stuck in the comfort zone and those in the challenge zone. Taking our passion and dreams and making them happen is the difference. When you enter the challenge zone, your dreams take action and you become a doer and not just a dreamer.

Jeff had certainly taken action over the last year and made progress with his hitting and fielding. He was hitting .348 going into the last regular season game. He had only one error at second base and helped break the infield record for double plays in a season at their school. His determination and focus were contagious. The coaches felt great about the team's position as the season wound down. However, off the field there may have been issues of concern. When Debbie initially talked to Jeff, he got a little defensive and didn't believe what he referred to as "rumors" about the baseball team. He knew if the stories were true, their dreams would be shattered!

Gretchen's mission to get the whole team more engaged in practice (into the challenge zone) was a successful one. This isn't always the case for some as the effort to do so can be a frustrating experience. Nothing difficult is ever going to be easy but it is always a worthwhile endeavor to try to motivate others. Gretchen remembered how close she was to quitting because her frustration was getting the best of her. Her efforts were appreciated. The athletic director stopped Gretchen in the hallway at school and praised her for her impact as a leader after they won the section championship. The soccer team was on their way to the state tournament for the first time. The challenge zone is full of great surprises.

In 2006, the storage building on our challenge course had a huge banner posted on the side of it with our theme, *"Match your efforts with your dreams."* When I ask athletes who wants to get better at their sport. They all raise their hands. Unfortunately, most remain in the comfort zone. Athletes in the challenge zone are constantly taking the initiative to do things they know will make them better. They don't wait for coaches or anyone else to tell them what to do. They know what will improve their physical abilities or skills and they don't procrastinate in doing what needs to be done. Effort, intensity, exertion, and sweat are appropriate words for the challenge zone. If you enter the challenge zone, don't expect it to be easy.

Discovery Zone:

Entering the discovery zone isn't something you decide to do; it is a result of time well spent in the challenge zone. It happens because of hard work, determination, and focus. It is that time when you achieve the next level of performance you have been striving for or even beyond. The discovery zone is similar to finding treasures and closely linked to learning to celebrate progress. It is like a well-deserved vacation. The purpose of a vacation is to refresh someone and build confidence for the next endeavor. It might be a few minutes or a few days. The discovery zone energizes and provides the motivation to get back to work, just like a vacation. When you discover what you're capable of doing, you open doors to a higher level of performance.

Ashley told Jill she needed a vacation and Jill joked about going to Hawaii after the state meet. She knew that wasn't going to happen but she also knew Ashley was right. Jill was exhausted and needed a rest. For her, it was never that easy. She over-trained often and was stressing over decisions about college. Ashley reminded Jill that rest is an essential part of training and offered to take her and the two other senior gymnasts out for pizza and laser tag. Since Jill looked like she was losing weight, Ashley had been a little concerned about Jill not eating enough, or the possibility of an eating disorder. When Jill consumed nearly half of a large pizza, she figured she didn't have to worry.

Sometimes our discovery experiences can lead to more than we imagined. In volleyball, it is a necessity to stay behind the ball when attacking it. This seemingly small adjustment produces some very significant results: the ability to hit the volleyball harder and the ability to see the block. Seeing the block is significant in many respects. In 1986, I had the opportunity to tour Peru, Venezuela, and Ecuador with USA Athletes in Action men's volleyball team. While in Peru, we played the Taiwanese National Team and got beat up bad. They killed us at the net, but it was an incredible learning experience for me. It didn't seem to matter if we had a block up in the right spot or at the right time. They were able to hit it off the block in some way, shape, or form every time. When I returned from that trip to South America, I made it a mission to take that part of my own game to the next level. I spent countless hours practicing my hitting with towels hanging over the net, hitting gaps and seams. I'd put tape on the dividing drop curtain in the gym in order to work on hitting specific pieces of tape after tossing the ball to myself and jumping up to hit it. I learned to enjoy hitting against more than one blocker and to use the block to my advantage, which helped considerably when I played teams by myself. Every sport has treasures waiting to be discovered! Spend time in the challenge zone and your time will come.

When you read about the zones, it is more than likely that you did some self-reflection. In addition to determining which zone you are in, it is important to understand the power of influence. If you spend a lot of time with someone, they're moving in one direction or the other. Those around you influence who you are and you influence who they are. Be a leader and bring others with you to the challenge zone.

PART II

THE THINGS THAT

WILL MAKE YOU

OR BREAK YOU

Chapter 9

RECOGNIZE

YOUR

OBSTACLES

Obstacles are seldom welcome, even when they only slow us down a bit. Who hasn't encountered annoying detour signs? I recall being on my way to a training session and coming upon a *road closed* sign. Most of the time there are well-marked detours established, but not that day. Obstacles are obvious to a driver, but not so obvious to an athlete. It would be helpful if there were road signs in the gym like; "CAUTION – NO ONE AT WORK!", "BE PREPARED FOR LACK OF MOTIVATION," or "NO FOCUS ZONE AHEAD," "WATCH OUT FOR DRAMA." The challenge zone has obstacles like no other zone. Dealing with those obstacles is what makes the challenge zone what it is - challenging! I've become sensitive to this issue. Why? Many athletes don't think about what is holding them back. It is crucial to understand what will help take us to the next level and, at the same time, be aware of what could trip us up, slow us down, or keep us from reaching our goals.

"Ready Aim" is one of the top three games I do for sheer entertainment value alone. Ultimately, it is blindfolded dodge ball with a minefield mixed in. Each athlete has a partner. One person is blindfolded inside a specified area and the other is outside the lines directing their teammate to a soft ball. They also help them avoid touching the cones and hula-hoops (land mines). If the player on the inside touches one of the land mines, they're done. If the blindfolded person finds a ball, the objective is to throw it at one of the other blindfolded competitors. In the midst of people throwing balls at each other and trying to avoid the minefield, I represent the "evil forces". I tell them that I like to "help" people too, but make it clear that I am the "evil forces."

When the game starts, it is loud! Those on the outside are shouting directions to their partner on the inside. Some don't listen to their partner and touch land mines right away. A few hide in the corners hoping others will eliminate each other. I gain some trust by giving participants balls, but follow up with a cone. Those playing or those watching, sometimes laugh so hard they cry. This game provides a smorgasbord of applications to athletics: teamwork, communication, trust, focus, strategy and adjustments. Many athletes don't consciously recognize their physical or mental obstacles. One of the main reasons I implement this game into any training agenda is because it is a great platform to discuss obstacles.

When I think of the word initiative, I think of people who recognize opportunity and seize the moment. They don't just *think* about doing it, they *do* it. Take the following story about chickens for example. It is a simple math problem with a twist of initiative. I grew up on a farm with 10,000 'laying hens'. Chickens would sit in the windows along the length of the barn. We figured they enjoyed watching us play baseball in the field. One day there were five chickens sitting in a second level window and three of them decided to fly out of the window in order to get a closer look at the game. How many chickens remained? Are you guessing two? Good math, but that isn't the right answer. I did say there were five, and then three of them "decided" to fly down, but that doesn't mean they "did" anything. Our society is full of people who "decide" to do something, but never follow through.

Many athletes don't think about what is holding them back.

Most employers, coaches, and parents would agree that initiative is becoming a lost art. I've wrestled with this issue for a long time and still haven't been able to reach any definite conclusions. Bear with me for a moment as I try to explain. Some people don't even notice things that could or need to be done. For them, the prospect of "taking the initiative" is not a possibility since they can't take action on something they are not aware of. These individuals are either in the dead zone, or have dug their heels in the comfort zone and don't seem to want to go anywhere.

The opposite of taking the initiative is procrastination. Before Olivia started hitting against their garage door, she became aware of what she had been doing through a song on the radio called, "*It's One Thing To Say It*," by Al Denson. She wasn't listening very closely, but part of the lyrics from the chorus jumped out at her:

> *It's one thing to say it*
> *It's another thing to do it*
> *We've got to take what we believe*
> *And live it oh live it*
> *It's one thing to say it*
> *It's another thing to do it* *(See resources)*

Olivia knew right away she was procrastinating with tennis and conditioning. She was always "talking" about what she was going to do, but never getting around to doing it. She was very frustrated with herself at the time, but was glad she had done something about it. Her only regret she was having now was that she didn't start earlier.

In athletics, the majority of athletes could tell you one, two, three or more things they could do to enhance their abilities, but rarely do them. For example, many athletes know that flexibility would enhance their performance and recovery, yet they don't work on it. Consider my own testimony. In 1982, I was the Assistant Strength and Conditioning Coach at St. Cloud State University in St. Cloud, MN. I helped create training programs for athletes. Before they started lifting weights I would tell them to stretch, but I never paid attention to their technique and didn't offer suggestions. I had my doubts about the perceived benefits of flexibility and whether or not flexibility could be improved.

In spite off my uncertainties, I wanted to challenge myself, so I did some research. Stretching is a skill that should be developed. Athletes need to learn how to stretch by feeling, not just distance. In other words, they need to learn how to listen to the muscle and adjust the stretch tension accordingly. Not only does flexibility enhance athletic ability, it does wonders for recovery time and improves an athlete's longevity. As an older athlete, believe me. I developed my flexibility and plan to maintain it for the rest of my life. Flexibility is certainly one of the more neglected components of training from a physical standpoint. Many movement skills initiate from the abs and few athletes take the initiative to work on their abs. Core strength is a link between upper and lower body strength. Sure, everyone wants six-pack abs, but in athletics, core strength serves more of a functional purpose. For things like flexibility and core strength, you can often take the initiative without facilities or equipment.

(Messing around with Ty)

For a few bucks, you can find a decent hacky sac and take the initiative to improve your footwork, foot speed, and agility like Olivia did. If you worked with a hacky sac five minutes every day, imagine what would happen.

When I worked with a college softball team they huddled up before the session to hacky to each other. Later in the session, they were trying to accomplish something very difficult that involved hacky skills (but using a big ball). They refused to resort to a creative (easier) solution and were determined to reach their goal. When time ran out, I decided to leave the big ball there for them because I knew they would work on it. Getting athletes out of the comfort zone is about getting them to do those one, two, three or more things that would make them better. What is holding you back?

Jeff knew the team had a great shot in post-season play. That is why he felt such disappointment. He hoped what he heard about Josh's drinking were rumors, but decided to confront him anyway. The coach had already talked to Jeff about the three guys: Josh (shortstop), Eric (pitcher), and Lance (right field). The two other guys owned up to the choices they made and would be off the team for two weeks, but initially Josh denied everything. Jeff felt a strong sense of responsibility to do something, not because he was the captain, but because he and Josh had been good friends since they were in 5th grade. Josh had always said that he would never drink because his dad was an alcoholic, but here he was, doing exactly what he said he wouldn't do, at the worst time ever! Josh admitted his drinking to Jeff and told him he felt terrible about letting the team down and that he, Eric, and Lance would miss the first play-off game.

Jill had signed with a Division I College after the state meet. Now she was back in the gym working hard. She probably would have chosen a school in another state, but her mom wanted her close to home. Everything was going 'fine' until her dad caught her throwing up again. The first time she didn't know he was home and she just told him she didn't feel well. He didn't think anything of it. However, the second time she tried to make excuses but started to cry when he pressed for some answers. Jill confessed that bulimia had taken control of her life for more than a year. She admitted needing help as it was affecting her entire life, and especially her performance in the gym. She took one big step towards recovery when she acknowledged that she needed help. She had tried to quit so many times on her own, but it didn't work. The family went through a great deal of heartache, but set up a treatment program at a facility specifically focusing on eating disorders.

Our choices, behavior, and lifestyle patterns can become our greatest assets or our biggest obstacles. We may be surprised to find out how much of our daily life consists of patterns and habits. Changing routines is not easy. Early on I mentioned that the average American spends nine years of his or her life watching TV. Think about how those figures would change if you added computer and smart phone time. Distractions are everywhere! Our priorities need to be well-grounded; otherwise, we'll be caught off guard. If we're not careful, obstacles turn into excuses. The more we make excuses the better we get at making them. For more than 30 years, I've listened to excuses. The most popular one is, "I don't have time!" It is amazing what we **do** have time for when we **don't** have time.

Some obstacles may be the result of life circumstances or other people. We may not have any control in some situations. Several guys on the basketball team had already talked to Brad about his dad. Brad woke up at 3:00am only to find himself replaying some of the things his dad had yelled out from the stands at the game the night before: "That was a stupid shot," "Set up," "Get down on defense." What he said to officials was even worse. It had been more intense since his mom stopped coming to the games. In the past, his dad would only yell out things related to Brad, but now he was yelling at everyone. The guys were playing tentatively and worried about facing the "wrath of Jim." It was affecting the entire teams' performance. The next day, Brad was relieved when the coach informed him that the athletic director had called his dad to tell him that the officials' union said they wouldn't send officials to their games if Jim's behavior continued. As I mentioned early on, one of the ugliest things in sports is a parent living their life through their kids.   It creates such unnecessary pressure and can be a huge obstacle.

The key is recognizing obstacles that could be avoided. Many injuries could be prevented with proper preparation. For example, many athletes use plyometrics in training without developing an adequate strength base. Then they wonder why they have shin splints. What about the runner who logs too many miles in training and then wonders why he has a stress fracture? I believe many athletes desire to start the season in the best shape of their lives, but don't foresee their obstacles. They have good intentions, but it is hard to take it to the next level without recognizing what <u>might,</u> or what <u>is,</u> holding them back.

Gretchen wished she had recognized a potential obstacle before the state soccer tournament.   Along with her teammates, she was encouraged by all the well-wishers before going to the tournament. The school even hosted a pep-fest to send them off. Everyone wanted them to win and Gretchen knew they had a shot if they played their best. After winning their first game 2-1, they came up with the motto, "In it to WIN it." Unfortunately, that didn't happen. In their next game, they were beat by an opponent who didn't compare to the two teams they had beat in the section playoffs. What happened? Within ten minutes of the start of the game, they had a couple of great shots on goal and the other goalie made a few incredible saves. No one verbalized it, but they started thinking they were not going to be able to score and slipped into the panic mode. The game was over before they knew it. They never did score, losing 1-0.

The next few chapters are devoted to looking at some of the things that will make you or break you. Even if you don't feel you struggle with some of these potential obstacles, read the chapters just to be encouraged that you're on the right track. No one in sports performance is excluded from the influence of work ethic, dealing with frustration, setbacks or negative self-talk, communication, fear, choices, and leadership.

Drama has become an issue in almost epidemic proportions. Just envision a coach rolling his eyes and saying, "Oh my gosh, drama! I've had enough of it." I hear it too often. Guys are not immune to drama but it seems that if guys have a beef with someone, they'll usually make it clear face to face, without saying much to anyone else about it. Girls on the other hand, will often tell everyone on the team except the person they are talking about. On top of that, too many are willing to listen to it without asking, "*Have you had a chance to talk to her about it?*" Many times, it has nothing to do with the sport, but rather about someone's boyfriend or girlfriend, a comment about what someone wore at school, or something posted on social media. The possibilities are endless.

Drama could pertain to playing time, a bossy captain, or how someone "looked" at someone else wrong during the game, practice, or in school, etc. Not long ago, I worked with a dance team with some real drama issues. The team had chosen captains for the year in the spring (several months before my training). One of the senior girls who wasn't selected as a captain was still bitter and angry. She wasn't at all shy about her disapproval, with EVERYTHING! Standing with her arms crossed, then hands on the hips, rolling her eyes, etc. The body language was bad enough, but then she started with the negative comments, "That is a dumb idea!" "Why would you do that?" "I knew that wasn't going to work!" At that point, I pulled her aside and asked her how she thought her comments were helping the team. Did she know how cancerous her attitude was and was she really trying to destroy the team's motivation? She looked like she wanted to be mad at me, but instead she started to cry. The coaches were glad that I said something to her and I just hoped it would make a difference.

The key is recognizing the obstacles that can avoided.

There is unnecessary drama associated with "playing time." At the varsity level in high school, grade level typically has something to do with it. One of my biggest pet peeves in sports at the varsity level is athletes who feel a sense of entitlement because they are upperclassmen. Often they do the bare minimum in practice or the off-season, but feel they should be starting or playing more just because they are upperclassmen. Too many times, the drama is created when parents get too involved when they are uninformed about what goes on in practice or the off-season. The objective at the varsity level in most athletic programs is to put the best team out on the court or field. Coaches working with the younger athletes typically try to give everyone playing time, but not necessarily equal time.

At the foundation of drama is self-centeredness. Drama is an enemy of teamwork since it strongly contradicts what teamwork is all about. Drama becomes a HUGE obstacle for any team at any level. How do you avoid it? I would love to say there was a simple formula that would end drama, but there isn't. However, I feel there are steps you can take that will help reduce the chances of drama negatively affecting your team.

1. First, be proactive. Meet with the whole team and parents (if possible) at the beginning of the season. Talk about how drama is

a threat to a team, but only has as much power as we give it. Drama works like cancer. Even a little bit of drama is dangerous because you know the potential it has for spreading. Eventually it can destroy you if you don't wipe it out. If it is only caught after it has already spread, the chances of stopping it aren't as great. When you hear rumbling of drama, do what you can to stop it! Most athletes/teams along with coaches and parents want to have a fun and successful season. You don't have to have a two-hour workshop on it, but take time to at least recognize it for what it is. Talking about the destructive nature of drama *before the season* will make a big difference in reducing or even preventing it.

Instead of waiting until drama occurs and reacting to it, being proactive is more effective and can play a big part in reducing or preventing drama. Address drama issues right away with the athletes involved with effective communication. Often coaches assume it will just "go away" but it may only get worse. If you don't feel qualified dealing with it, consider tapping into counseling services provided through the school or university.

2. Many of our parents have drilled the following statement into us, "If you can't say something nice, don't say anything at all." That may be some of the best advice we were ever given. I've already mentioned my only rule for teambuilding is "no put-downs" but this should go beyond practice and competition. Counseling materials focused on improving relationships will recommend couples assume the best about each other. We often jump to conclusions when we don't know the facts. On a team, it can be tempting to say something about someone else if we are upset with them. Remember, we don't improve our own reputation by trying to destroy someone else's reputation. We need to examine our motives when we say anything negative about someone.

3. Have you ever heard these words of wisdom? "He who listens to one side of a story is a fool!" Drama needs an audience and can't flourish without someone who will listen to it. Those who will listen fuel the drama queen who thrives in the presence of drama. It's like going fishing and waiting for something to take a bite (listen to their drama). After a while, if they don't get any bites, they'll give up! Make it a team rule, DON'T listen to it.

There is nothing better than a DRAMA-FREE season!

The list of potential obstacles is endless. Everyone encounters them. Some are just circumstances of life. Encountering obstacles is inevitable, but a key to taking your performance to a higher level is recognizing or even anticipating obstacles. A marathon can wear people out or even discourage a runner, but it is often the little piece of lint, balled up in a shoe, that throws people off. Learn to recognize those tiny things that could hold you back, or throw you off course.

Chapter 10

HARD WORK

PAYS OFF!

Hard work beats talent when talent doesn't work hard. There is no substitute for hard work. Obsession is a word the unmotivated use to describe the dedicated. These statements are more than words used by many. They are the truth. An unwillingness to work hard is definitely one of the biggest issues keeping athletes from achieving their potential and entering the challenge zone. I have already mentioned that many coaches frequently express this concern saying, "They want to win, but they don't want to work. They want to be champions, but don't want to train like champions." Too many athletes fail to see the connection between hard work and the desired outcome. They fail to recognize that when the time to perform comes, the time for preparation is GONE.

Several years ago I took a head coaching position at a high school that had a struggling volleyball program. In the middle of the season, we had a match scheduled with a rival team. When the day arrived to compete, the girls were excited. I thought they had played a great match, but their excitement was gone when we lost the match in five games. In fact, most of them were in tears. I was curious why they were upset and asked, "What's wrong?" They said they wanted to win, to which I then responded, "When did you decide you wanted to win?" They looked somewhat confused by the question, but one of them said, "Well, we wanted to win tonight." I knew that but I still asked, "Have you been working really hard in practice lately?" They dropped their heads and said no without any hesitation. At that point, I just mentioned that they may want to think about that long before the event if they "really" want to win. It was a great teachable moment and made a difference in practice later on.

Gretchen's team didn't have much time to recover from the emotional upset after the semi-final. She hoped they would be in the right frame of mind for the 3rd place game and the coach's post-game speech helped. Even though the coach didn't have an extensive soccer background, he was putting in a lot of extra time learning the game and he was a motivator. He said he would only be disappointed if they hung their heads or didn't show how well they could play in the next game. Gretchen thought about the previous season and knew she would have laughed if anyone had told her the team would be in this position. It would be a great life lesson about hard work for everyone on the team.

My mission in this chapter is to change the damaging misconception that hard work isn't fun and something to be avoided! This isn't just about athletics; it's a cultural perspective towards hard work. Too many people want things and opportunities handed to them without doing what is necessary to acquire them. This perspective is baffling. I challenge just about every team I work with to think about it. I tell them, "Don't take my word for it, just look around and watch people. Whether it is in practice, the classroom, or watching people working at a store or restaurant, you'll find this to be true. The people who are working the hardest are having the most '____'." I've never have to give the answer away. Everyone always knows the answer is FUN! Why is it that we tend to avoid hard work, when everyone knows that those who are working the hardest have the most fun!

When reminiscing about athletic days, it's more than likely you have heard someone say, "We could have been so good if we had only worked harder." So many people regret not giving everything they have in many areas of their lives. For some time Brad had been haunted by thoughts of regret, but he used those thoughts as a pleasant reminder he was on the right track now. He had never had so much fun playing basketball and the coaches were thrilled with his transformation even though they were reluctant to believe the 'new' Brad was there to stay.

Brad was relieved that the athletic director had called his dad to talk to him about his behavior at the games because he thought he could then avoid that confrontation. However, the more he thought about it, the more he realized the situation created the best opportunity to tell his dad how he was feeling. When he told his dad about the pressure he felt from him and the embarrassment caused by his behavior, tears welled up in his dad's eyes and ran down his cheeks. Brad had never seen his dad cry before and it meant a lot to him that his dad apologized. No one was more excited than Karen since she figured she could start going to the games again. The team was 21-3 with only a couple of games left in the season. Everyone was pumped for playoffs and Brad was excited that all the hard work was paying off.

I understand the concept of avoiding things in life that aren't fun. Who *wants* to go to the dentist, get a shot, or have a flat tire? Who *wants* to go outside in Minnesota when it is 32 (F) degrees below zero? Recently on such a day, I stopped to fill up at a gas station early in the morning. The window cleaner was frozen solid in the wiper fluid container. All the schools were closed for the day - Governors' decision. Changing a flat tire in temperatures like that would definitely be something to avoid since frostbite occurs within minutes of exposure. However, avoiding the hard work associated with athletics is a mystery to me. It is like the '*Eighth Wonder of the World*'. Why wouldn't an athlete want to work hard? Remember, we know that the people working the hardest are having the most fun. Those who are slacking off, taking the easy route, or doing as little as possible aren't having much fun. They are not very successful and they never find out what they are capable of doing.

Jeff felt like they had lost their opportunity to show what they could do after three of the guys were suspended for chemical violations through the first game of playoffs. Losing a pitcher with a 1.36 ERA and an all-conference shortstop going into the playoffs wasn't the ideal situation. While Jeff was busy moping around, Debbie said, "Is this really how you are going to respond to this situation?" "What else can I do?" asked Jeff. Debbie had already thought about a response and was glad he asked. "You are forgetting what got the team this far: hard work and determination. I realize you and Josh rock at turning double plays but don't you have confidence in the other guys who could step up to the challenge? You are reacting instead of being proactive." Jeff got the point quickly and forgot to thank Debbie for her words of wisdom. Within five seconds, Jeff was on his cell phone. He called the coach asking if he would be willing to hit ground balls to the infield players after practice the upcoming week. Jeff contacted the rest of the infield about his plan and was excited to get to work.

Being able to train in an intense fashion is to be treasured. When I was conditioning for volleyball, I tied myself to the volleyball poles with surgical tubing on our sand courts. I would do resistance training with agility patterns, sprints and movement skills until my legs felt like rubber. I'd pick the hottest time of the day to work on jump serves and hitting drills because I wanted to be ready. I wanted to train harder in practice than I would ever have to play while competing. Then I knew I would be ready. I loved it!

Olivia couldn't wait to get home to tell her mom. The varsity coach was at the field house that night with his two little boys playing catch with a football and shooting baskets on the other end of the facility. He was glancing down at their court as Olivia and Marci were playing, but Olivia assumed he recognized her from the distance. When he and the boys came around the track, they stopped and he said, "Olivia, is that you? I can't believe how much you have improved! Your serve looks awesome!" Olivia wasn't the only one feeling proud. Marci had always wanted to coach, but unfortunately her work schedule since she graduated from college didn't allow for her to do so. To her, watching Olivia working hard and making progress was a priceless gift.

The people who are working the hardest are having the most FUN!

One of my favorite challenges related to hard work is 4-Way Tug of War. It is nothing but hard work. Instead of traditional tug of war, four teams pull in four different directions. On a basketball court there is a cone in the four corners that the person on the end of the rope needs to grab. The teams compete against each other instead of working together like most of the team building activities. I tell them to think of three teams they compete against that they most like to beat. Even after two minutes of intense pulling, seldom does a team get to the cone, unless one or more of the other teams just gives up or loses the footing. The question likely asked following this intense challenge is "Does anyone ever win?" The second most asked question is "Can we do that again?"

In case you are curious, the longest I've ever let a team continue tug of war was 23 minutes and 27 seconds. Ten minutes into it, I was so impressed with how hard they were willing to work that I said, "Let's call it a draw. I'll give everyone free t-shirts for working so hard." I assumed everyone would say, "SWEET" but they said "NO WAY". They were not giving up. Thirteen minutes later, someone finally got the cone. By that time, there were several guys whose calluses on their hands had ripped open. There was blood all over the ropes. It was awesome! I had to throw the ropes away, and ¾ inch New England multi-line is not cheap rope.

Years ago, I did this challenge with the Minnesota Golden Gophers Women's Hockey Team (National Champions). About a minute into the challenge, one of the athletes yelled out, "This is impossible. No one is ever going to win!" My response was, "Go ahead, you can quit; just drop the ropes". When I said that some of them did actually drop the ropes, but as soon as they dropped the rope, they realized that not everyone was quitting so they went back at it. If I gave each group of athletes' unlimited time, obviously someone would eventually get to the cone. Think about the characteristics describing a team that would win: determination, hard work, teamwork, strategy, strength, communication, perseverance, etc. My favorite response, however, is "the team who wants it the most". In the competitive realm of athletics, "who wants it the most" is not about beating a team that you really want to beat. Who wants it the most is about the off-season, preseason, every single drill in practice, and every single minute of practice. It is about creating a habit of intensity; giving everything you've got, not some of the time, but all the time, mentally and physically. When you enter the practice, you make a choice, "How hard are you going to work?"

Hard work is a choice that eventually becomes a habit. When you establish the "habit of intensity," you are in business. When athletes begin LOOKING for things they can do to take it to the next level, they start drawing a connection between *dreaming* of doing great things and actually *doing* them. Think of your favorite inspirational movie. It is likely to contain elements of hard work.

Preparation and hard work are the keys. I like to ask athletic teams the following question, "How many of you started this season in the BEST shape of your life?" Often no one says anything. There is dead silence for a second or two. Occasionally, an athlete has trained hard and that athlete rarely says anything because someone else will say, in a joking sort of way, "Oh yeah, Jamie." Unfortunately, it is an exception, rather than the rule. Starting a season in the best shape of your life would be the first sign that you are in the challenge zone, ready to work hard and have fun.

Many athletes think they are working hard, but could be giving so much more if they were motivated. Some parents think their son or daughter is working hard all the time, but they may hear a different story from the coach. I was fortunate when I coached that I had virtually no conflict with parents. However, one set of parents were relentless about their daughter's playtime as a senior. Her parents thought she was working so hard. Not only did she not condition in the off-season, she did very little in practice! I don't even recall her breaking a sweat! I told her parents they were MORE than welcome to come watch a practice. They never came. If you are a high school coach, I'm sure you can relate to this story.

Years ago while in Indianapolis, I did a series of school assemblies for five days with some other incredible performers. After completing a program the last hour of school in a large high school, I stayed for an evening session. Having retreated to the staff lounge to read for a while, I got up to take a stroll. Walking by the coliseum-like gymnasium, I noticed one light on in the middle of the gym, so I peeked in. On the other end of the basketball court, someone was running the stadium steps. I stood in the doorway for several minutes and just watched. Sprinting up, coming down, sprinting up, coming down, etc. I walked across the basketball court and met her as she came down the stairs. Her gray t-shirt was completely drenched and sweat was dripping from her chin and nose.

I said, "Gosh, you're training hard. What are you working out for?" "Track" she replied. This was the beginning of February. I mentioned that I was from Minnesota and asked her if they were already involved in the Track & Field season. She said, "No, the season doesn't start for another month." I told her how impressed I was that she was training with this type of intensity all alone in the "off-season". I was curious, so I asked, "How do you do in track?" She replied, "I do ok." I could tell she was humble so I pressed her a bit, saying, "Come on, tell me specifically, how do you do?" Only then did she say, "Well, last year I won State in the 100 and 200 meter." The first thing I thought, "Gee, I wonder why?" There she was busting her butt in the off-season, training with that level of intensity. Hard work? Oh, yes! However, to her, probably not. When you find someone who has a "**Burning Desire**" to take it to the next level, hard work doesn't seem like hard work.

Sometimes progress in athletics isn't just about working hard physically. It might be about doing hard things: confronting a teammate about choices they are making, supporting someone who is starting when you would love to be, maintaining a positive attitude when things aren't going as planned, etc. For years, Jill had worked so hard in the gym and the results followed. Training hard physically seemed easy compared to the things she needed to do for her treatment. A critical part of treatment is family involvement in order for the whole family to experience healing through growth and change. She would need to have a heart to heart conversation about her feelings with her mom. It was one of the hardest things she had to do, but at the same time one of the best things she could do for herself in recovery. Jill was encouraged when her college coach made a visit to the treatment center. She was excited about what she was learning and anxious to get back to the gym to work hard with a different frame of mind.

I have been teaching Elementary Physical Education for a long time. Once in a great while, I'll have a day when I don't feel like working very hard. Have you ever had one of those days? Those days DRAG on and are never very fun. However, if you work hard and are committed to what you do, time flies because you're having fun.

Do not be led astray. Hard work ROCKS! It's the key to taking your performance to the next level! Hard work needs to establish roots and a solid foundation, otherwise, the winds of complacency will blow us right back into the comfort zone. Look into stories about people who have been successful. Someone observing may think, "Oh, that person is so talented!" However, once they start digging into the athlete's history, they find nothing but hard work. This is true in life. Take your passion and make it happen. Match your efforts with your dreams. It won't happen without hard work!

Chapter 11

FRUSTRATION:

DON'T LET IT GET

THE BEST OF YOU

One of the most destructive obstacles for athletes at any level are the negative tapes that play inside their heads. Negative self-talk is destructive because our internal dialogue is the foundation of mental toughness. So many student athletes literally talk themselves out of doing things they are capable of doing in their sport or in the classroom. Experiences from the past play a big part in how we talk to ourselves. These experiences also have a HUGE influence on our performance. We all develop roadways of thinking. Mental pathways can become valuable tools, or nasty habits. For some athletes, negative self-talk is like a roadblock with no alternate route. This occurs most often when we're challenged, get frustrated, perceive something as impossible, or encounter setbacks. Negative self-talk will keep us from putting in our best effort. There is no doubt about it, if we challenge our limits, we will get frustrated. Frustration isn't a bad thing, but if we don't respond to it appropriately, it can become a nasty obstacle.

Everyone hits a fork in the road. I call it the frustration factor. How we respond when we get frustrated is the key to success. The patterns of thinking, when frustration sets in, become powerful habits. What goes on inside our heads is crucial in setting the stage for the degree of success we'll experience when frustrated. If we take the wrong road, it is a dead end. If we start thinking, "this is too hard," "I'll never be able to do this," or "I'm such a loser," any sense of determination will be derailed. If we shut down, give up, or throw in the towel our effort may drop off the face of the earth. When frustration gets the best of us, it is like hitting a brick wall. Many athletes would be amazed if they caught a glimpse of what they are truly capable of but never find out because of negative self-talk.

How we respond when we get frustrated is the key to success.

We can think faster than we can talk. A lot of information (positive or negative) can fly through our head in seconds. The first step in changing negative self-talk is recognizing it for what it is and understanding its destructive power. I have one rule for team building. It has been the same for more than ten years. "No put-downs." Most athletes assume this rule applies to what they say to their teammates. If someone on your team makes a mistake, the last thing they need is one of their own teammates ripping on them. When this happens, their teammates take on the role of the "other" team.

Guys are typically more verbal with their put-downs. The female gender is much better at giving the "look." Most agree that they learn the "look" from their moms. When it comes to "no put-downs," the most important person in that rule is you! Some athletes are extremely good at putting themselves down. They don't need anyone else to help them out. They're doing a good enough job by themselves. Monitoring our internal dialogue is so important. Throughout the day, we have all kinds of conversations inside our heads. We may want to determine if our internal dialogue is building us up or tearing us down.

I received a call from a gymnastics coach about a week after I'd done a session with her team. She said one of her younger athletes was on the balance beam in practice and, at one point, she stopped with a puzzled look on her face. An assistant coach asked what was wrong, and she said, "When Rick talked to us about positive self-talk, did he say we should do that inside our heads or out loud?" The coaches got a kick out of it. I was thrilled to hear she was applying the information from the training experience.

Whatever the reason for negative self-talk, discouragement is the by-product. Discouragement and motivation don't mix. Determination and negative self-talk don't mix either. It is like trying to mix oil and water. Discouragement is something that can so easily take control of our lives. Losing control can start with believing the lies associated with negative self-talk. Don't give up control.

For quite a few years, I wondered why some athletes are so BLASTED DETERMINED when frustrated, while others seem to give up on a whim. I believe the biggest factor is self-talk. Athletes with a high level of determination and persistence respond appropriately to frustration with positive statements going through their heads. They are able to maintain their determination, in part because the tapes playing inside their heads are positive in nature. Taking it to the next level is hard without the right perspective. We are more likely to talk ourselves out of a big step than we are a little one. Therefore, starting with small steps is important. Small steps generate momentum and create enthusiasm. Seeing things in parts and chunks makes the mountain so much more obtainable. Consider some of the statements below regarding self-talk and think about where you are with the tapes that play inside your own head.

* **Our self-talk will either cheer us on, or turn us off.**

* **Our self-talk either builds us up, or tears us down.**

* **Our self-talk will be one of our biggest fans, or our greatest opponent.**

* **Our self-talk either encourages us, or discourages.**

* **Our self-talk will cause us to challenge our limits, or limit our challenges.**

* **Our self-talk determines whether we live in hope, or despair.**

* **Our self-talk determines whether we live life to the fullest, or live life going through the motions.**

* **Our self-talk determines whether we reach for the stars, or crawl under a rock.**

* **Our self-talk determines whether we are looking to the future, or dwelling on the past.**

*   Our self-talk determines whether we are striving for more, or settling for less.

*   Our self-talk determines whether we lift our teammates up, or pull them down.

*   Our self-talk determines whether we reach our goals, or reach the bottom.

*   Our self-talk determines whether we say, "I can," or "I can't".

*   Our self-talk determines whether we are just beginning, or already finished.

*   Our self-talk determines if we decide the direction we take, or let others decide for us.

*   Our self-talk determines whether we are climbing, or falling.

*   Our self-talk determines if we have a vision of where we are going, or if we are lost.

*   Our self-talk determines whether we step up to challenges, or step back from them.

*   Our self-talk determines whether we help our team, or hurt it.

*   Our self-talk determines whether we build up our confidence, or plant seeds of doubt.

*   Our self-talk determines whether we are standing tall, or ready to fall.

*   Our self-talk determines whether we are in the challenge zone, or stuck in the comfort zone.

*   Our self-talk determines whether we run the race, or just watch it.

Our responses, perspectives, and attitudes will affect those around us. Most coaches would agree that one bad attitude could swing the whole team in the wrong direction. Attitude problems are often times directly related to our response to frustration.

Nothing hard ever comes easy. How a team collectively responds to setbacks is also crucial. One of my favorite team challenges is a marble & tube challenge. Each athlete gets a tube about 15 inches long and stands in a single-file line starting at the end of the basketball court. With 10-15 participants in each line, they try to get the marble to roll through the tubes without dropping it. There is tape at the ends of each tube that they aren't allowed to touch preventing them from grabbing the crease between the tubes. The objective is to see how far they can go without dropping the marble. If the marble drops, the team has to start over. The activity requires everything needed to be successful on the court or field: communication, focus, leadership, patience, and determination.

One high school boy's hockey team fell apart after several minutes working with the tubes and marble. Every time the marble dropped, they pointed fingers and blamed each other. This team was overly concerned about getting to the end of the court. Their verbal exchanges were negative. The challenge is always harder than people think. The point behind the challenge was not so much about going the distance without dropping the marble; it was about how they responded when the marble dropped. When I asked them how they were doing, they knew! The coach said afterwards that they respond the same way in games. It all comes down to attitude. Our attitude will determine our altitude. When your attitude is right, your abilities will follow in the gym, at home, at work, and in the classroom. The four main areas challenged with setbacks are as follows:

1. Focus – Focus is the ability to fix our thoughts on the task and eliminate distractions, maintaining concentration on the process without letting our mind drift and wander. Refer back to the Chapter Four on focus.

2. Intensity – It is all about our effort physically and mentally. We need to find creative ways to motivate ourselves and tap into reserves in order to give everything we have. When I think of intensity I can picture someone giving everything they've got!

3. Enthusiasm – This is the ability to stay fired up, despite circumstances. Maintaining a positive attitude is key. Be aware of the messages your body language may be sending. Many athletic slumps could be prevented by staying in a positive, enthusiastic frame of mind.

4. Determination – This is my favorite word! Determination fills the gap between where we are now and where we could be. Determination fills the gap between what we can do now and what we could do. Only when you are determined do you ever find out what you are capable of doing. The definition reveals the element of choice. Determination is a choice of the will.

Jeff and the rest of the infield had spent at least five hours after practice in one week working on developing rhythm, timing, and communication. Losing Josh at shortstop was definitely a setback, but Jeff accepted the challenge and did what he could to prepare the roster for each game. Andy settled into the position well and only had one error in the last two regular season games. Everyone was excited for him when he hit the first home run of his high school career to tie the playoff game going into the seventh inning. Jeff ended up with the game-winning hit. After the game, Jeff thanked Debbie for her willingness to challenge him to be more proactive to the situation at the end of the season. Jeff's role as a leader made an impact on the whole team.

Brad may never recognize how his response altered his life. It would have been easy for him to quit when the coach confronted him early in the season. Sometimes the truth hurts. Many people rationalize and justify their bad attitude and never face the truth head on. Brad's transformation from one of the team's biggest obstacles to one of the team's greatest assets was a highlight in 27 years of coaching for Bill.

When some athletes have setbacks, their determination crumbles, along with their focus, intensity, and enthusiasm. When others have setbacks, they seem to be able to bring their focus, intensity, enthusiasm, and determination to another level. You can't go back and change the past, but changing your attitude can change your future. You're on the road to success when you come to grips with the fact that setbacks are only detours. Make the most of every detour in your life.

Make the most of every detour in your life.

You may have thought going into treatment for an eating disorder would have been a huge setback for Jill, but she felt encouraged and empowered. Her patterns of thinking had changed so much that she found herself welcoming the situations that left her feeling helpless and out of control in the past. She was pursuing a degree in psychology with an emphasis on counseling. After her experience in treatment, she knew where she wanted to work when she graduated. In the gym, it was back to business as usual. Outside the gym, Jill felt much more focused without having to fight the constant battle with bulimia. She felt such freedom and that freedom would not have come without treatment. At treatment, Jill fell in love with riding so her parents bought a horse named "Costa" for her graduation gift. Costa played a big part in her recovery.

Mistakes are inevitable and athletes certainly respond differently to them. Since mistakes are inevitable, we need to view them as part of the process in taking our performance to the next level. Your choice -- you can either learn from them or let them get the best of you. Our perspective is powerful. The worst mistake anyone can make is being too afraid to make one. Athletes prone to playing negative tapes inside their head are likely to have an unhealthy perspective towards errors and receiving correction. Often they learn absolutely nothing from the experience because they are so busy feeling like a loser. Because of this, too many athletes don't want to find out what they need to adjust; therefore, they avoid seeking information related to their mistakes and don't find solutions.

Marci noticed Olivia's response to mistakes rather quickly, possibly because she could see so much of herself in Olivia. At one point when Marci was about to share a tip with Olivia about her backhand, Olivia pulled the dreaded hand up in the air, and said, "Stop!" She didn't want to hear what she was doing WRONG. It didn't even matter how it was said, her interpretation of constructive criticism was "I am losing, so therefore I'm a failure." Marci waited until they were done playing to talk to Olivia about it. She told Olivia that she often wondered how good she could have been if she would have been more coachable when she was younger. "Losing doesn't mean you are a failure, but failing to learn from your mistakes is the biggest failure of all." Olivia knew Marci was right so she asked, "What were you going to tell me about my backhand?" Marci replied, "Oh no, never mind," but Olivia persisted, "No, really, I want to know." After Marci gave Olivia some pointers, she told Olivia she was glad she really wanted to find out what she was doing wrong.

Some athletes are able to forget their mistakes, while others keep a mental log of every mistake they've ever made. After an athletic event, they are able to recall all the things they did wrong and the mistakes they have made, but can't seem to recall all the things they did right! This is a counterproductive attitude and has a detrimental affect on confidence. An athlete can easily establish a negative sub-conscious mind that can hinder her performance. I mentioned in Chapter Two that the mind makes more mistakes than the body. This is often the subconscious at work. I don't believe some athletes or teams collectively see the power of this. I've seen teams who talk themselves out of beating other teams. They might even be ahead in a game, but they find ways to lose. So much of it has to do with the tapes that play inside our head. Recognize and change it!

If we see mistakes as a negative thing, we inhibit our ability to take our skills to the next level. Some people may feel that we should forget our mistakes and I agree if their perspective is a negative one. The key factor in learning is to utilize the information obtained from experience in the development of higher-level skills and seeing it as a positive. Coaches often tell me they don't feel their athletes are listening and that they need to say the same things hundreds of times. With the proper perspective on the learning process, a coach's insights are priceless and more than welcome. It is unfortunate that many athletes have an "I don't want to hear it" mentality when it comes to their coaches offering tips or insights regarding their performance.

We are more likely to excel when we view mistakes as golden nuggets instead of big red check marks. Mistakes are details that enable us to improve, with the right perspective. Think of them as GIFTS! If someone gives us a gift, we are grateful, especially if it is something we can use. An athlete with the proper perspective about mistakes is a treat for coaches to work with because they are so much more coachable. With free-style kayaking, I love it when I find out what I'm doing wrong so when I make the necessary adjustments I know it is only going to help me take it to the next level. I felt the same about volleyball after playing so many years. When I found things I could improve during a performance, I couldn't wait to get to the gym to work on those elements of my game.

One of the first steps in changing negative self-talk is recognizing it. The negative tapes usually start playing when frustration sets in. Frustration isn't a bad thing, but how we respond to it is very significant. How do you respond when you get frustrated? The list is endless obviously, but my intent is to draw attention to reasons primarily linked to performance and achievement:

I was talking about the whole concept of frustration in one of my elementary PE classes. I was curious to find out what kind of awareness these young students had on the issue. After a few minutes of discussion, one boy raised his hand, and said, "Mr. Rassier, this is physical education, not frustration class." Many of the kids thought it was funny, and it was. I said, "Jason, that's a good point. Maybe we should have a class called "frustration class 101". How many of you would really like to learn how to deal with frustration?" All the kids raised their hands!

There are many questions regarding frustration and negative self-talk that may never be answered. We do know that the way we think when confronted with frustration will produce powerful habits if done repeatedly. People often talk about the "road to success," but fail to realize how many get lost because they take the wrong path when they hit the fork in the road called the frustration factor.

Who would think success would create adversity, but it happens often if the whole team isn't on the same page. Gretchen didn't feel there was an issue until she received top player in the area, was selected All-State Team, and had several college coaches contact her. Megan, one of her friends from the team, wouldn't even acknowledge her in school, even if Gretchen tried to talk to her. Word got back to Gretchen that Megan was going around telling people that Gretchen thought she was so much better than everyone else. Actually, Gretchen had thought very little about herself and had done so much for the team. Most of the girls were grateful for the experience they had during the season making the trip to the state tournament, but envy and jealousy had gotten the best of Megan. It went on for several weeks, but gradually fizzled out when Megan couldn't get anyone to take on her perspective about Gretchen. Initially, Gretchen was hurt and felt like retaliating, but after a long visit with Ella, she was convinced it had nothing to do with her and she was glad she wasn't pulled into the drama.

Achievement and failure are powerful and rewarding things. The same is true for progress and setbacks. There is nothing like the sense of accomplishment and the satisfaction and pride of a job well done. I love stories of others who have overcome adversity and made the most of their situations. Participation in athletics provides priceless life experience. There are many forks in the road for all of us. Which road will you take? Have you ever wondered about achievements that have never occurred, progress never made, or attitudes that were never changed? How we respond to frustration, setbacks, and adversity is definitely a key to taking your performance to a higher level.

Chapter 12

--- FEAR ---

THE GREATEST

INHIBITOR OF

PERFORMANCE

Fear can be a huge obstacle and a huge motivator! Fear causes us to do things we shouldn't do and keeps us from doing the things we should be able to do. Fear is unavoidable. One difference between successful and unsuccessful people is how they handle those pressure situations. How do you perform under pressure? There are people who perform better and those who perform worse under pressure. If it were 10% better or 10% worse that would be a 20% swing – one way or the other. For some it may be even higher. What creates that pressure? Fear! What are we afraid of anyway? In athletics, it could be a number of things:

- Fear of failure

- Fear of not being the best

- Fear of injury

- Fear of making a mistake or blowing it

- Fear of making a fool of ourselves

- Fear of not meeting someone's expectations

- Fear of letting our teammates down

- Fear of success

- Fear of losing

I would estimate that more than 90% of athletes in competitive situations are performing in the state of fear. I've played many volleyball teams that should have destroyed me, yet I watched them beat themselves because of the fear factor. For me, it was fun playing in the moment, while they were consumed with concerns about the potential outcome – they were afraid of losing. There are sports in which the fear of injury is more predominant. I've had many conversations with athletes, coaches and parents about how a past injury can disable athletes, despite the fact that they have completely recovered physically. However, the tapes playing inside our heads can produce crippling effects until they are replaced with a sense of confidence and visions of successful performance.

The baseball team got ready for the next game. Everyone was excited about having the whole roster back in uniform. Josh, Eric, and Lance were able to practice during their suspension time and were ready to go. The playoff game was a big one for Jeff's team. Their opponent had two solid pitchers both of whom had signed full-ride Division I College scholarships. A year ago, Jeff would have been losing sleep thinking about facing the pitcher they were matched up against. It might have been the fear of striking out several times, or possibly the thought that he didn't even belong in the batter's box against that pitcher! Last season he threw a no-hitter against them. With the time Jeff had invested on his swing and learning to read the pitcher, he was looking forward to the opportunity. Jeff's preparation produced confidence which went a long way in keeping the fear factor from influencing his performance. He felt like he had the advantage and tried to get the team in the same mindset. With a .382 team batting average and three guys hitting over .400, Jeff figured they were more than ready for the challenge.

It wasn't until after her first two gymnastic meets in college that Jill even noticed what had changed for her in competition. She looked forward to the meets and no longer worried about disappointing her mom. She felt a sense of freedom without the grip of fear playing a part in her performance. Much of the pressure she felt from her mom in the past was unfounded, since her mom only wanted her to do well because she felt Jill really wanted to do well. The disappointment Jill felt from her mom was only her mom feeling the disappointment that she believed Jill was feeling. Both of them wished they had figured that out long ago, but were able to make the best of the misunderstanding.

Not only does fear affect performance, it keeps many of us in the comfort zone. A friend of mine once purchased over $1500 in whitewater kayaking equipment, but never got back on the river after a scary experience. He failed to get his roll, had to do a wet exit and swim a few times. If he had spent a little more time practicing his roll, he may still be kayaking. Preparation goes a long way in keeping fear from disabling us. Most fear in athletics comes from our concern about the outcome of a game, match, race, meet, or performance of any kind. I wanted to establish the difference between the pursuit of excellence and the pursuit of winning early in the book since it is such a factor in the ability to perform at the highest level. The bottom line is this - if you are overly concerned about the outcome, it is unlikely that you'll perform at the highest level and it can take the fun right out of your performance. The more you are able to dismiss thoughts about the outcome, the more fun you'll have. When you are having fun, it changes a pressure situation into a fun one.

If you are overly concerned about the outcome, it is unlikely that you'll perform at the highest level and it can take the fun right out of your performance.

Teams who visited our challenge course split their four-hour experience into two segments. We did the low initiatives on the ground first, and then the high elements which involved putting on a harness and climbing. When teams sat on benches around a fire pit, I would give them a 'heads up' on what they would encounter during the training. Since we followed the universal "challenge by choice" rule, no one was ever forced to do anything.

When explaining the high elements, some would squirm in their seats. The high elements were a great way to get athletes to see how fear could affect their performance. There were times when some of the potential participants were immobilized by just the thought of getting up on one of the elements. F.E.A.R. could be an acronym for False Emotions Appearing Real. Even if I mentioned that hundreds of people had gone across the catwalk or one of the other high elements without an accident, it didn't take away the fear. Many things can play a part in forming an unrealistic fear response. Do you tend to see the positive or negative side of things? How we perceive our future and our past sets the stage for how we respond at any moment. With most fears, negative self-talk is lurking around the corner.

More than once, I was on the zip-line platform with someone who couldn't get themselves to step off. I had established a repertoire of suggestions over the years to encourage people to take that step out of the comfort zone. When they would finally go for it, they would scream with excitement on the way down and many would run back yelling, "I want to do that again!" Fear so often holds us back from experiencing the exhilaration that comes from getting out of the comfort zone.

The high element that probably caused the most fear was the "Leap of Faith". The participants would climb a pole then walk out to the end of a platform six feet long and about a foot wide. From there they would jump off the platform and attempt to grab a trapeze bar suspended from a cable in front of them. A football player who weighed at least 300 pounds (solid) walked out to the end of the platform. His legs were shaking so much that the whole platform started to shake. He backed up three times to the pole just to try to regain his composure. Eventually he was able to jump, but was not able to grab the bar because he grabbed on to the climbing rope connected to his harness. The last summer we were open we had three bathroom related accidents on the leap of faith. It is hard to perform your best when fear gets the best of you.

It is hard to perform your best when fear gets the best of you.

You may not see an athlete's legs shaking, but fear can have a devastating affect on an athlete's performance. Parents and coaches play a significant role in an athlete's mental state when it comes to the "Fear Factor". Sometimes parents or coaches put too much emphasis on winning, and it creates the fear of losing. The fear of losing may be one of the greatest inhibitors of athletic performance. One of the ugliest things in sports is parents living their lives through their kids, or coaches living their lives through their athletes. Most parents and coaches do an incredible job, but all of us have seen it, even at the elementary level. Comments and non-verbal reactions can affect athletes' performance and even affect their desire to continue pursuing the sport.

We put so much emphasis on winning; it creates the fear of losing.

You may remember that "In it to WIN it" was Gretchen's team motto going into the semi-final match at the soccer state tournament. Gretchen didn't think much about it then, but now she couldn't stop thinking about the psychological implications of the team motto going into the game. She wasn't upset over the loss anymore, but wanted to learn from the experience. The semi-final game was a blur and Gretchen couldn't remember much about it because they had slipped into the panic mode. However, she could replay much of the 3rd place match in her head. Their perspective going into that semi-final was "we have to win" as opposed to the 3rd place game where it was more "what do we have to do in order to perform at the highest level." Gretchen realized that their strong desire to win had created the fear of losing and it became their biggest obstacle.

Bill knew how Jim's (Brad's dad) behavior at games affected the performance of the team. Even as the coach, he found himself thinking about the comments made from the bleachers. Jim had cleaned up his behavior from a verbal standpoint since he had received the warning from the athletic director; however, the players had grown accustomed to watching him make such a spectacle of himself. It was difficult not to notice Jim's looks of disgust, eyes rolling, arms crossed, interlocked fingers behind his head, and standing up with his hands on his hips. When things were going well it was no problem, but in tight games, the message was loud and clear. The result? The players (including Brad) seemed apprehensive about every dribble, pass, or shot. They would second-guess themselves, which meant missed scoring opportunities and unnecessary turnovers. They would fall apart because of the fear factor.

Some people may dispute this, but I feel the mark of a great coach in not having to talk about winning very much at all. When the emphasis is placed on the pursuit of excellence, athletes become more concerned with how they are playing than on the outcome of an athletic event. They are able to think and play in the moment, instead of letting fear get the best of them. Winning is a great goal; however, if it becomes the main thing, fear will choke out the ability to focus. Fear and focus are nearly incompatible with each other. A few of the things that can happen when the fear of losing sinks its ugly claws into athletes are:

- They lose their rhythm
- They lose their timing

- They lose their touch

- Negative self-talk kicks in

- Their self confidence dwindles

- Doubt enters into the picture

- Their breathing can be affected

- It takes the fun out of a sport they should love

- They lose their ability to relax

- They lose their ability to stay focused

- They get tense and tight

- They have increased sweating and dry mouth

- Their heart rate and blood pressure are elevated

- Their ability to visualize is distorted

- They lose the ability to anticipate what their opponent will do

- They start playing in the panic mode

- They are unable to think and play in the moment.

The effects on performance can obviously be devastating. Just the thought of tryouts for the varsity tennis team made Olivia's heart race and her hands sweat. The coach had seen her several times at the field house during the winter season and even told her she had a great chance at making the varsity team. When spring came, she would wait for the boy's team to finish practice so she could get on the court. She had stuck to her hacky sack routine in addition to working on core strength, cardiovascular conditioning, and some weights to improve her shoulder strength. What was she so afraid of anyway -- that she wouldn't play very well, not make the team, get too nervous to play, or do something embarrassing? Marci reminded Olivia that preparation is the best way to beat fear and that Olivia had done everything she could to be well prepared. Marci shared a story with Olivia about her sales job. She would always get so nervous for big presentations and learned that it was because she felt unprepared. She told Olivia, "If you prepare and study for a test, you look forward to taking it because you know you are ready. When August comes you will be ready!" Olivia appreciated Marci's words of encouragement. The next time she thought of tryouts, she actually felt excited about showing what she could do.

The worst part of the fear factor is how it takes the enjoyment out of sports. My goal as an elementary physical education teacher is to get students to love sports and games and embrace a fitness lifestyle for the rest of their lives. I've seen too many athletes stop participating when it is no longer fun. Fear isn't always the problem, but I believe it is often the source of problems that go unrecognized.

In the beginning of this chapter, I talked about performing under pressure, 10% better or worse. If we take some time to look at the list of how fear can affect us, think about how even 1-2% can change your performance for the better or worse. It can make the difference between a "clutch" performance (performing your best when you need it the most) and "choking under pressure." Wouldn't you rather be the clutch performer? How do you perform under pressure? Knowing how you respond under pressure and understanding why are important keys to performing at a higher level. Look at the questions below to gain some personal insight.

On a scale of 1-10 answer the following questions:

How do you respond when the pressure is on?
1 2 3 4 5 6 7 8 9 10
Calm, cool, collected. Total panic mode

What happens to your self-talk under pressure?
1 2 3 4 5 6 7 8 9 10
Positive, confident. Negative, doubt

How often do you think about making a mistake during a performance?
1 2 3 4 5 6 7 8 9 10
Never happens   Always happens

How do you respond to a "mistake" during a performance?
1 2 3 4 5 6 7 8 9 10
Calm, cool, collected. Total panic mode

How often do you start thinking in terms of "what if..." before a game?

1 2 3 4 5 6 7 8 9 10

Never happens   Sometimes   Always happens

Would you want to take a shot at the buzzer, or be up to bat with bases loaded, two outs, and tie game?

1 2 3 4 5 6 7 8 9 10

Always   Maybe   Never

Several key steps are huge in combating the impact fear has in the athletic realm.

1. Having the right frame of mind regarding the pursuit of excellence (Chapter One) is foremost. When we are more concerned about winning the game than we are about learning the game and having fun, something is wrong. We can't pretend to not be concerned about the outcome. It doesn't work that way. Our passion to improve has to be genuine. I shared how this mindset brings the performance to the highest level and winning becomes more and more likely, but the sheer desire to win isn't the motivating force. Remember the college basketball coach who thought that if winning wasn't the main and only thing, an athlete's effort would diminish? Nothing could be further from the truth. When the emphasis is placed on the process and not the outcome, fear loses power. The more we develop this state of mind the less likely it is that fear will affect our performance and the more fun our performance becomes.

2. From Chapter Two through Chapter Ten the emphasis was placed on how we can take our performance to a higher level. Learning to set goals, celebrating progress, developing focus in practice and performance, having a performance vision, understanding the steps of learning, understanding the zone we may be in, recognizing obstacles and working hard all play a huge part in this journey and are all a part of the preparation process. When we invest in preparation as athletes, it only helps in developing confidence in our performance. A more confident state of mind is less likely to fall prey to the fear factor.

3. Pay attention to the tapes that play inside your head. Closely related to confidence is self-talk. I run the risk of repeating myself from the last chapter, but some things are worth repeating. Negative self-talk is often the culprit for many struggling with fear. So many of us talk ourselves out of performing at the level we are capable of when the negative tapes start playing. The more we can replace the negative self-talk with positive tapes the less likely it is that fear will affect our performance. Awareness is the first step to changing our tapes, but it isn't an easy process since many of us have developed some nasty patterns in our thinking and break the "no put-downs" rule.

Those three steps are BIG steps. They are components of athletics that need constant attention, but our discipline in maintaining the right perspective in each of the three areas is necessary to keep fear from becoming a negative force in our lives. Keep pushing for the next level and show what you can do!

Chapter 13

DEVELOPING

LEADERSHIP SKILLS

I don't think anyone would dispute the importance of leadership. Without someone "leading" what direction does a team go? Often times, nowhere. Some athletes have not experienced the impact of a teammate who is a strong leader. When working with teams, it doesn't take me long to pick out the leaders. It doesn't take long to recognize teams who are lacking leadership either. Lack of leadership is obviously a huge obstacle. Successful teams have strong leaders.

Regardless of what your status is in terms of leadership, this chapter pertains to you. If you aren't leading, you're following and it may be a good idea to consider who is influencing the direction you're heading. The 4-way tug-of-war mentioned in Chapter Ten applies here. Life is like a tug of war with everyone being pulled in different directions. It may not feel like a fight because patterns and habits are well established. However, it is important to identify what may have influenced your life patterns and habits. It may also be important to decide if they fit the route you want to be going. At this point in the book, you know Olivia, Brad, Jeff, Gretchen, and Jill pretty well. How has leadership affected them?

Olivia didn't have the mindset of a leader but she was definitely following. Marci had become somewhat of a mentor in her life and the results were quite different than if she would have followed the influence of Bridget, who had no goals, wasn't doing well in school, and was boy crazy. Tennis was teaching Olivia to focus and it was making a difference in the classroom. Olivia's mom was thrilled and never complained about driving her to practice.

Brad had developed great leadership qualities throughout the season. That may not have been the case if he would have listened to his friend Greg. Greg had some choice words to say about Brad's coach when Brad was given the ultimatum to quit the team or take a week off to decide if he was on board with the team. Brad remembered thinking to himself that maybe it was exactly what he needed and it became a turning point in his life. We all have turning points in our lives that represent a tug-of-war. A strong leader often creates those turning points in others' lives and influences their direction.

Jill's experience on the college team was fantastic and it had everything to do with the team captains. From the moment she stepped on campus, she felt at home because they made her feel a part of the team and were willing to answer questions about the campus. The captains taking the initiative to welcome her in so many ways took away the intimidation for Jill being on such a big campus.

Jeff's impact as a leader was a factor in the team's improvement from a 10-12 record the previous year to an 18-4 record at the end of the regular season. Building the team's confidence played a big part in their victory in the semi-final game. Jeff had heard Josh was still drinking and confronted him about his choices. Josh said everything was under control but Jeff was not convinced. He told Josh to call him anytime he was tempted to make a poor choice and offered to just hang out or go to a movie. Jeff felt a strong sense of responsibility as a leader to help not just Josh but everyone on the team stay on the right track on and off the field. He truly put action into the word leadership.

Given the coaching situation with the soccer team the previous season, Gretchen had become a student of the game and planned the majority of practice time. Other than a little drama with Megan after the season, the whole team had caught Gretchen's vision of what they could accomplish and it **changed everything** in practice. Gretchen had taken the initiative to do little things during the season that went unnoticed, but each had made an impact. Her experience during the season was something she never would have learned from a book. Future college teams were considering her partly because of her leadership abilities.

Most coaches would agree that success often hinges on the strength of leadership. The title of "captain" doesn't mean anything if the captain's leadership is weak or even non-existent. Everyone is eligible to be a leader. There are many great resources available exclusively on leadership. The information below will help you with ideas for your own program.

The leadership training I do with athletic teams and corporations is experiential-based, but I'm excited about what this chapter could offer on paper. I hope you're challenged to take action in at least one specific area as a leader. Awareness of your program's leadership status is important. Just like the earlier chapter on the steps of learning, part of developing leadership is becoming aware of things that could or should be done as a leader and then doing something about it.

Many want to make an impact and be the best leader they can possibly be, but they aren't sure what that entails. Listed below are some statements about leadership. Some require action and others represent character traits of a strong leader. Don't read these statements too fast. Think about the implications of each statement. Read them several times. Great Leaders:

- ❖ Need to have an intense desire to take their performance to another level and bring the team with them. Passion persuades.

- ❖ Do not try to get others to think *highly of them*. Their desire is to get others to think more *highly of themselves*.

- ❖ Make an impact by **taking the initiative**. Nothing stays on the to-do-list for long. They certainly "get 'er done." The best leaders don't think about whose responsibility it is or if they would get *credit* for doing it, they just do it.

- ❖ **Establish trust: they don't demand it**. No one will follow someone they can't trust. Control freaks don't produce teams, they destroy them.

- ❖ Need to be willing to **serve others** and lead by example.

Great Leaders:

- ❖ Have a unique way of **engaging others in the process**: getting them to come up with ideas, solutions, or take the initiative without depending too much on them.

- ❖ Need to be honest with themselves. Understanding their strengths and weaknesses is the first step in becoming more effective leaders. Check out the leadership test in the appendix.

- ❖ Make meaningful connections with teammates who may not be their friends. An example of this is when a talented senior connects with and encourages the least talented underclassmen.

- ❖ Have strong core beliefs and place **high value on integrity**. They do the right thing even when no one is watching.

- ❖ Understand coaches' expectation for practice, competitions, off-season training, and meetings.

- ❖ Are **mentally tough** in the competitive environment. They are able to maintain determination, enthusiasm, focus, and intensity despite the circumstances. They recognize the impact their role as leaders has on others' attitude and frame of mind.

- ❖ Demonstrate the willingness to **invest** in the team. They are often the first to arrive or the last to leave. Because of their **strong commitment** to the team, they are often the hardest working.

- ❖ Need to take responsibility for any wrongdoing. They don't make excuses or try to blame anyone else for their mistakes.

- ❖ Ask for help and are open to insights and opinions of others.

- ❖ Are readers. Reading right now is a good sign!

- ❖ Need good communication skills.

- ❖ Learn to tactfully confront teammates about issues that may be affecting the team.

- ❖ Make the effort to arrange activities and events for the team or sports program at all levels outside of practice and events.

Great Leaders:

❖ Recognize the destructive nature of negative self-talk and do not allow teammates to put each other down. They look for ways to encourage and strive to establish an encouraging environment.

❖ Make the effort to arrange activities and events for the team or sports program at all levels outside of practice and events.

❖ Celebrate progress and **recognize** effort and improvement. The encouragement makes others want to do more and better.

❖ Have a **vision** of performance and outcome goals and work to develop that vision in others. They know that to achieve the vision you can't be going through the motions in practice.

❖ Help direct others, not push them. They say, "Let's go," not "Go." Real leaders are able to light a fire in their teammates, not under them.

❖ Demonstrate the pursuit of excellence academically, as well as athletically.

❖ Are passionate about their sport. They organize and participate off-season conditioning and practice.

❖ Need to be emotionally stable. When a leader pouts or whines they lose credibility. Leaders set the tone for how others will respond to circumstances.

❖ Will often determine the quality of the program.

❖ Understand that "leadership" is not a title -- it is an active position.

❖ Make good choices regarding alcohol and other drugs. They have the desire to be a positive influence on those around them.

The list could be overwhelming, but not if you want to make an impact. Leadership is a big responsibility. Some coaches select captains and others don't. Some coaches have athletes vote for captains, but many say it becomes a popularity contest. Other coaches may have voting, but they make the final decision. The title does not necessarily make anyone a leader. Many coaches have told me that their best leaders were not even captains, but rather other athletes who stepped up and made an impact as leaders. It may be the best athletes, or someone who isn't even a starter.

In sports, athletes given the responsibility of "captain" are either making a difference, or just filling a position. They are either bringing the team to the next level, or watching them fall. In athletics, there is no plateau – either a team or program is making progress or going downhill. Who can make the biggest difference? A strong leader!

Chances are you have stories about great leaders. I hope you have had an experience with a model leadership mentor you would like to emulate. Learning from an example and leading by example are both great concepts. The word lead is an action verb. Take the initiative to do things that will make an impact as a leader. When people see that you are the real deal and are willing to serve others they will follow. As the old saying goes, "you have to walk the walk and talk the talk". If your life inspires your teammates to achieve more, you're a leader.

If you are in a leadership position, everything preceding this chapter should have prepared you for it. Growing as a leader is an honor and great responsibility. It will change you, your teammates, your classmates, your school, your family, and the rest of your life. Many companies look for people to employ who have been involved in athletics. Why? The athletic experience is priceless. Athletics is the ideal classroom for learning life skills such as teamwork, goal setting, communication, dealing with frustration/setbacks/adversity, focus, confidence, work ethic, leadership, choices/consequences, and making the most of your ability. I hope this chapter has made you think about who you are following and who has motivated you to become all that you can be as a leader.

Chapter 14

CHOICES

ARE POWERFUL

Taking your performance or your life to the next level starts with choices. Each preceding chapter, in some way, has to do with choices. Your choice to pursue excellence, set goals, be focused, work hard, and recognize obstacles will hopefully become habit. Choices lead to habits, and habits become your lifestyle. Good choices create momentum and stimulate a desire to celebrate progress. When that happens, you will surprise yourself with what you can do.

Regardless of the amount of natural ability you may have been blessed with, you'll never achieve your potential without making good choices. Poor choices only jeopardize your potential, as well as the team's potential, whether amateur or professional. A strong commitment generates good choices that may not be related to how you feel. A lack of commitment generally produces poor choices. For example, when the alarm clock goes off for an early morning workout, you may not 'feel' like working out but you do it because you are committed (and you know you'll be glad you did).

Brad and Gretchen's commitment to their programs made an impact. Brad's choice to be on board with the mission of the coaching staff inevitably led them all the way to the section finals in the playoffs. The three previous years the team had lost in the first round of the playoffs. Brad had averaged 18.6 points a game during the season and set a school record for assists as well. He had truly become a "team player." He was already looking forward to the next year's basketball season as a senior.

Gretchen had developed into the ideal leader through many of the choices she made during the season. After narrowing down her options, she visited two different colleges. The first visit turned into a major disappointment when the captains of the university soccer team took her 'out' to the bars to 'show her a good time' after the campus visit. It was quite the contrast to the next visit where the captains told Gretchen that over the past two seasons the team had decided to be a "dry team." Gretchen was excited about being part of the college program. Her plan was to pursue an elementary teaching degree with a coaching minor.

When Jill sought help through treatment, she never thought of working with people struggling with eating disorders. She often thought about how her choice to get help had changed her life. Because of the positive impact treatment made on her life, she pretty much made up her mind to pursue a counseling degree when she graduated. She was enjoying her college gymnastics experience and had gone to nationals as a freshman and sophomore. It remained to be seen whether or not she would pursue the Olympic dream.

Choices lead to habits, and habits become your lifestyle.

Besides choices related to conditioning and skill development, everyone makes a choice about mood-altering substances. This chapter will focus primarily on the choice to be chemically-free. In my personal background, I mentioned that I used the "One Man Volleyball Team" format as a platform to share a drug-free message in school assemblies. I'm passionate about helping young people make the best choices. That passion may have started when I was in high school. During my sophomore year in high school, I played saxophone in bands. It was a great way to earn money on weekends. As a musician, I saw just about everything. Some things were entertaining, and others downright depressing. Just picture an intoxicated newly married couple throwing punches at each other on the dance floor. What about a bride making out on the dance floor with one of the groomsmen and the groom not being very happy about it? Do you think alcohol was involved? What a sad way to start, or end a marriage. The consumption of alcohol can create awful memories.

I'm lucky to be alive after driving home between 1:00 - 4:00am nearly every weekend for seven years playing in bands. I still have a vivid picture in my mind of a motorcycle driver's body laying about 60' from his bike. He had taken a curve too sharply and hit the driver's side of an oncoming truck. Later reports revealed his blood alcohol level was nearly double the legal limit. I witnessed a number of fatal car accidents. Tragedy for everyone involved! I guarantee you'll never find anyone who says, "Gee, I wish I would have spent **more** money on alcohol when I was younger... that was such a good investment!" Sadly, it doesn't take long to find people who talk about how lives were lost or destroyed because of using drugs.

Jeff knew there must have been something wrong when the coach called at 8:00 on a Saturday morning and asked if he could stop by. Jeff pretty much knew what the visit pertained to before the coach showed up and was already regretting not doing more after he confronted Josh about his drinking. His gut feeling was right on, unfortunately. Josh had rolled his new car at 1:30 that morning and was in intensive care at the hospital. He had a punctured lung, four broken ribs, and a fractured collarbone. Josh's troubles were not just physical in nature since he would also have to deal with consequences of DUI (driving under the influence) charges.

Jeff was devastated, not only because they would obviously miss Josh in the game that afternoon, but he felt that he could have prevented it from happening. The coach reassured him that no one could be responsible for other people's choices. Jeff had already done all that he could. It wasn't good timing with the game that afternoon. The team struggled emotionally but still won the section final game 3-2. It was a bittersweet moment for the team but they all went to visit Josh in the hospital after the game. In the state tournament, they lost their first game, but ended up taking the consolation championship. They wondered how things might have been with Josh in the line-up. Josh would get help, but he would never forget what he missed his senior year of high school.

After a program at a middle school in Ohio, the principal came up to me and pulled a large coin out of his pocket. He said, *"You know Rick, I didn't have my first drink until I was 25 years old, but I've spent the last nine years trying to pick up the pieces of the life I destroyed for the next 25 years. I lost my wife and I lost my kids. I think about it all the time. I'd do anything to go back to that day when I took that first drink and make a different choice.* " That large coin symbolized his nine years of sobriety. I still remember him telling me he wished he would've heard my message when he was in high school.

We don't always know what shapes the choices we make. For some, the health class at school may have affected our decision to abstain from alcohol and other drugs. For me, it was what I saw when I was in the band as I specifically remember deciding then that I did not want to drink ever in my life. That decision to be chemically-free was one of the best choices I ever made. Back in Chapter Nine I spoke about the blindfolded dodge ball game. The cones and hula-hoops represent obstacles, some that can't be controlled, and some that can. We have the power to make the best choices. Every time we do, it gives us more power. Every time we make good choices, we eliminate obstacles in our lives. Every time we make poor choices, we add to the minefield of our own lives.

We have the power to make the best choices.
Every time we do, it gives us more power.

I realize that what I say about drinking can be offensive to some people. If you're an adult, this may be a difficult chapter for you to read, depending on if you agree with the concept of being chemically-free. All I ask is that you think about this message before reacting or get defensive. Don't throw the book away because of my perspective on this issue. I feel the bottom line is that we, as adults, send some incredibly powerful mixed messages, but really don't want to look at the impact and influence our choices have on kids around us. If you are a student, people may influence your choices, but you have the power to make your own choice. Just remember how one choice can change your life.

I'm not saying if someone drinks or uses tobacco, they are a bad person, teacher, or coach. I'm saying that the **best choice** is to not use. Our society does not want to see the connection between the choices adults make and the choices kids are making. Check the statistics. If a parent smokes, it is more likely that his or her own kids smoke.

A big part of the denial comes from our inability to view alcohol for what it is -- a drug. Pay attention to how alcohol and other drugs are separated when people speak and write. You are much more likely to hear someone say, "alcohol and drugs" than you are to hear them say, "alcohol and other drugs". Why not just talk about "drugs" and know alcohol is included since it is our number one drug problem? We don't say, "apples and fruit?" We might say, "apples and other fruit." Maybe it is just semantics, but personally, I think it goes way beyond that.

Our society does not want to see the connection between the choices adults make and the choices kids are making.

As the advisor for a high school drug-free team, I had heard about John's drinking from some of his peers and teammates. I found several opportunities to talk to him, especially since he was an athlete. I received a call from John's mother. She was upset that I talked to him about choices and that I told him he *shouldn't* be drinking. Even though it was almost 20 years ago, I can hear her words as if it was yesterday. She said, "If you keep telling John not to drink, he is going to do drugs!" If you aren't thinking to yourself, "WOW," you may need to read her statement again. "If you keep telling John not to drink, he is going to do *drugs*!" She didn't think of alcohol as a drug. What makes it even more amazing is the fact that part of the reason I had been talking to John is because, as a junior in high school, he already had three DUI's. He was lucky he hadn't killed himself and fortunate he hadn't taken someone's life on the road.

Alcohol is so socially accepted that young people often think everyone drinks. Visit with any adult who doesn't drink and you'll find out how backwards our thinking is on this issue. People assume one of two things if you don't drink as an adult: either you are very religious or you are a recovering alcoholic and you *can't* drink. It is almost as though you have to have an excuse for not drinking. Think for a moment how ironic that is. Why should anyone have to explain why they aren't using a drug that is messing up so many people's lives? It should be the other way around. Interesting perspective, isn't it? The people who are using alcohol should be the ones who need to come up with an explanation. Unfortunately, when I tell students that I've never had a drink of alcohol in my life, they initially think I'm kidding. Isn't it sad young people would react this way?

After a "One Man Volleyball Team" presentation at a school assembly, a student approached me. It was obvious something was wrong. He looked like he was on the verge of tears. This junior two-sport athlete said he never had a drink, but felt like he was the ONLY one! He shared how much pressure others put on him to drink. As he was talking to me, he started sobbing. This was clearly something that bothered him. I felt for him and was disturbed that anyone should feel that way when he was making the BEST choice. How crazy is that? Courage is standing alone in the midst of opposition and making the best choice. His positive choice may help others make the same choice.

**Courage is standing alone in the midst of opposition
and making the best choice.**

Before someone turns 18, think of how many commercials they see telling them that if they drink, they are going to have more fun, more friends, and fit in better. I wish each of those commercials were longer. I wish they were hours, days, weeks, and years long so they had time to show what happens to so many people when they choose to drink. What happens on the road is bad enough. Alcohol-related crashes are devastating, but so many of the other issues go unrecognized. It is staggering how many very committed high school graduates head off to college only to completely waste the first year or two drinking. Binge drinking on many college campuses is completely out of control. I could throw all kinds of statistics out at this point, but that just doesn't work. No one ever thinks they'll be one of those statistics.

If you never use drugs, you don't have to worry about ever having problems related to alcohol, tobacco, or other drugs. The alcohol industry obviously doesn't want people making that choice, since it may hurt sales a bit. They came up with a great marketing scam that is very deceptive. You've heard the slogans, "Think when you drink", "Know when to say when!" and probably the most popular, "Use responsibly!" It defies logic. You can't use a drug you don't need and call it "responsible" use.

**If you never use drugs, you don't have to worry about
ever having problems related to alcohol or tobacco.**

The alcohol industry would love to have everyone drinking "responsibly". However, where are they when all the issues come up? Responsible use of a drug means using a drug that you need that is prescribed by a doctor. People try to justify their choices all the time and some of those choices affect the people around them. This may sound harsh, but if you are a parent or coach, think about the choices you are making. Your kids are watching! Everyone makes their own choice, but others influence everyone in some way. I'll never forget when my oldest daughter Gia was 2 years old and walked up to me as I was working on the computer at home. I had just taken a drink of soda and she looked up at me and said, "Daddy, drink, pop."

The gateway drugs are powerful. The biggest drug problem in our society is the fact that we don't call alcohol or tobacco what it is… a drug. So many young people think, "Oh, I'll just try it once." The most dangerous drink or smoke you'll ever take is the first one. If you look at the most popular New Year's resolutions, you will find two on every list: quit smoking and drink less. If you are young, do yourself a favor and never start. If you never take the first one, you never have to worry about the all the problems associated with using.

When we are young, we make choices that often stick with us for a lifetime. I've said earlier that choices lead to habits, and habits become your lifestyle. Some choices like fitness and reading are great choices that hopefully turn into lifelong habits. Other choices aren't so good. What do you do with idle time? If you get in the habit of turning on the TV now, you'll probably be doing it 20 years from now. Consider the choice to light up or take that first drink. I often ask students, "How many of you know someone who smokes or drinks who wishes they could quit?" You can imagine the response. Everyone's hands go up. It all starts with ONE choice. I have some great friends who are struggling with addictions, some who recognize it and some who do not. It is so important to understand the power and significance of each choice you make. If you are a student or young adult, I hope you are making the best choice. If your friends REALLY are friends, help them make good choices too!

Olivia was concerned about Bridget hanging out with the wrong crowd during the summer months so she spent a lot of time with her. The biggest accomplishment was getting her off the couch and out for volleyball. On the tennis court, Olivia was elated to make the varsity team. Marci was just as excited as Olivia was and she treated Olivia to her favorite restaurant. As a ninth grader, Olivia had grown up a lot in a year. She was involved in a group of students at the high school who made visits to the elementary school to talk about their choice to be chemically-free. If you do everything you can do to take your conditioning, skills, and abilities to the highest level, but fail to make the best choices and live chemically-free, you may end up losing it all.

More than ten years ago, I heard a story about two great high school athletes. Both of them were seniors and had full-ride scholarships to Division I colleges for their prospective sports. In the spring of their final year in high school, they went to a party and both of them were drinking. They thought it would be "fun" to play a game of "chicken" on their crotch rockets (motorcycles that you practically lay down on). They would drive straight at each other and whoever chickened out first would be the loser. Unbelievably, both of them won because neither one chickened out; tragically, they both lost their lives!

After learning the details of what transpired, I was amazed more at what *didn't* happen. Not one of their "friends" intervened and tried to stop them from doing what they were going to do. In fact, the atmosphere was more, "Wow, this is going to be cool" until the little game ended. The police report estimated that both guys were traveling at least 75 MPH when they hit head on in front of their "friends". Both of them died at the scene of the accident. That story is tragic! However, the story is being duplicated, maybe not in the same fashion, but all over the country. Young people make poor choices and their friends are sitting back saying nothing!

Every choice has consequences -- maybe not just for you, but for those around you. Some choices lead to incredible rewards and pay off down the road and others choices turn into a nightmare and may have some serious consequences. Make the choices that will bring your abilities and your life to the next level. Make the most of each opportunity. Things don't just happen, they happen as a result of choices. Every choice is powerful.

Copyright FACE 1993 (See resources)

THE 2-MINUTE

WARNING

I hope the end of this book is the beginning for you. Maybe this is the beginning of 'your' story, or you started a new story early on in the book when you began to apply the challenges. As you may have noticed the word graduation was added to this conclusion. This chapter is like a graduation speech. A graduation may be the end of something, but more importantly, it is the beginning of something else – something bigger and better. It doesn't mean you're done, just recognizing progress.

Your story may not have anything to do with sports. It might be about overcoming fear that has held you back for years, developing better study habits, taking your fitness/health to the next level, learning an instrument, pursuing a degree or a different job, kicking the smoking habit, or becoming more organized. Whatever it is that you do, you know the following statements apply:

1. Begin with small things, celebrate progress, and feel the momentum build.

Don't worry about winning or being the best. Acknowledge those baby steps and tiny improvements. Strive to get 1% better every day and watch what happens. If you pursue excellence, winning takes care of itself.

2. Watch out for little excuses. The more you make excuses, the better you get at making them.

It takes a while to establish habits and patterns in your life. Sometimes it is a fight for establishing the priorities that will help you achieve that next level and compromise is the battleground. In the beginning, do not rationalize or justify skipping something that is essential in achieving the next level.

3. Become an expert in recognizing distractions and potential obstacles.

One of the biggest challenges in taking your performance to the next level is recognizing what may hold you back or stop your momentum.

4. Celebrate progress! Do not compare yourself or your performance with anyone else.

Comparing yourself with anyone else may be the quickest way to let discouragement get the best of you. It is also unfair since someone may be more advanced because they have invested much more time than you have.

5. Make mistakes – lots of them! Learn from the mistakes and be willing to take risks!

People who excel in anything learn from their mistakes. Mistakes can be priceless teachable moments with the right perspective. Failure is part of the process.

6. Be persistent! Always get up one more time than the number of times you are knocked down.

Persistence pays off in many areas. Think of this word puzzle: (THHAERNGE) which is a three-word phrase within the group of letters. It would be good advice for someone who may feel like giving up. The answer is somewhere below. Try not to peek. Hang in there!

7. You don't necessarily have to know the future, but you have to believe in yourself.

Confidence is huge and self-confidence builds each time we celebrate progress. Worrying about the future tends to take away from our focus on the here and now. Trust that the results will come when you keep working hard.

8. Don't allow the negative tapes to play inside your head.

Remember: "No put downs" definitely applies to how you talk to yourself. Too many people talk themselves out of doing things that they are perfectly capable of doing. Develop a repertoire of response phrases for those times that the negative tapes start playing:
- That's not true!
- I love it when someone tells me I can't do something!
- I'm up for the challenge!
- Is that all you've got?

9. The harder you work the more fun you have.

You can't wish or dream outcomes into existence. Don't expect results if you aren't working for them. You will never regret giving everything you've got mentally or physically and you will have a blast doing it.

10. Learn to rest when needed and reward yourself.

More is not necessarily better if you end up over-training. Make sure you find proper balance. Use that vacation time that you earn in the discovery zone and take time to refresh. Put your feet up and then get ready to take it to the next level.

11. Pay attention to detail and make adjustments.

It is easy to do the "same thing" but doing the same thing gets the same results. Develop an eye for those details that make a big difference and make adjustments. Think of those details as treasures and seek them out. Get the most out of the time you invest and always look for a better way to do something.

12. Avoid skeptics who try to steal your enthusiasm.

Get used to other people telling you that you can't, or it isn't worth the effort. Treat them just like you would negative self-talk. I met a guy about a year ago who told me I would never be able to do a specific trick in my freestyle kayak. Actually, it only motivated me to even go way beyond that challenge. If I ever saw him again I would thank him for telling me that I couldn't do it.

13. Create opportunities, don't wait for them.

You may have heard the saying, "Good things come to those who wait." That might apply to waiting for a great meal out of a crock pot, fishing in a fish house on a frozen lake, or waiting for Christmas morning, but if you want to take it to the next level, you have to pursue it and create opportunities. It isn't going to happen unless you make it happen.

14. Watch out for the comfort zone.

You are either challenging your limits or limiting your challenges. The comfort zone will pull people in without them even knowing it. Satisfaction is a dangerous word. Many never find out what they are capable of because they slip into the complacency mode. It happens individually and as a team.

15. Develop the focus factor!

Remember focus is a skill to be developed. It is your ability to fix your mind on the task and tune out all of the distractions. Watch where your mind drifts since the more engaged you are the better your return on the investment of time. Remember that the clock tells it all: five minutes of focused practice is better than 1 ½ hours of going through the motions.

16. Celebrate progress and look back occasionally just to see how far you have come.

Sometimes people get so focused on long-term goals that they lose the sense of accomplishment that comes from celebrating progress.

17. Learn to use frustration as a motivator, not a terminator. Be up for the challenge.

How you respond to frustration, setbacks and adversity is the key to success. Be sure to monitor your determination, enthusiasm, focus, and intensity.

18. Take your passion and make it happen. Pursue your vision.

Long-term goals and vision are great, but they happen when you break that vision down into little pieces that can be reached today. Pursue parts and pieces of that vision every day.

* I can't remember, did I say anything about celebrating progress?

Did you figure out the word puzzle? I gave you the answer if you didn't notice. It was "hang **in** there." The word hang, was **in** the word, there. Persistence is an incredible character trait!

When working with a college women's basketball team, I did a challenge where the athletes needed to remember 23 steps on a big tarp with the coaches holding the map. They were not allowed to help each other so it took a great deal of focus and concentration individually. About five steps into the process, one of the athletes made a mistake and verbally put herself down. I heard her say, "I'm no good at this type of thing. I may as well give up!" I said, "Ellie, what is the only rule I have for training?" She said, "No put-downs." Then I asked her who the most important person in that rule was. She knew again, "Me" she said. I simply said, "Ellie, your attitude will determine your altitude" and walked away. Twelve minutes later, Ellie was the first one to make it to the 23rd step. The proud look on her face was priceless. When you change your perspective, you change your life.

I feel extremely fortunate to be doing what I love for my career and I'm excited when I see the results. Several years ago, an older man approached me at a restaurant and said that he was thrilled to see me again. Initially it was a little bit awkward since I had no idea who he was. I had done a keynote presentation for the custodial staff from schools, hospitals, etc. sponsored by a cleaning company. He was there and took the message beyond the work environment. He proceeded to tell me that he had lost 105 pounds after hearing my message and was now at his healthy high school weight from 34 years ago. He thanked me for changing his life, but I told him that I didn't change his life, he did. When you change your perspective, you change your life.

After a recent training session with a college swim and dive team, an athlete approached me and said, "I wanted to thank you for coming, but even more so, thank you for coming two years ago." He went on to explain how the last training session had made such a big difference in his training mentally and physically. He said that he would have never been a national champion if it hadn't been for the session two years ago. When you change your perspective, you change your life.

Think about the dreams that fall by the wayside and the New Year's resolutions that fade away. Too many give up on themselves. Remember that negative self-talk and determination don't mix and determination is the foundation of a disciplined lifestyle.

D	Determination
I	Initiative
S	Strategy
C	Commitment to Celebrate Progress
I	Investment of Hard Work
P	Passion, Persistence
L	Love & Leadership
I	Intensity
N	Next Level Obsession
E	Engaged & Encouraged

Maybe you have been procrastinating too long. It is time to let go of the past and write your future. This book is your spring-board to the next level. Take what you have learned and dive in!

APPENDIX

TAKE THE LEADERSHIP TEST

40 Essential Characteristics of Leadership:

Give yourself a score of 1-5 on each listing (1 being lowest)

Test #1

_____ Chemically-free

_____ Focused

_____ Motivated

_____ Good Sportsmanship

_____ Courageous

_____ Humble

_____ Confident but not arrogant

_____ Good role model

_____ Mature

_____ Respected and trusted

_____ Patient

_____ Selfless

_____ Friendly and caring

_____ Determined

_____ Disciplined

_____ Positive attitude

_____ Takes initiative

_____ Committed to team

_____ Cooperative

_____ Visionary

_____ Supportive and encouraging

_____ High level of integrity

_____ Accountable

_____ Lead by example

_____ Organized

_____ Strong communication skills

_____ Passionate and enthusiastic

_____ Sense of humor

_____ Charismatic

_____ SERVE others

_____ Innovative ideas

_____ Responsible

_____ Goal-Oriented

_____ Hard Worker

_____ Forgiving

_____ Consistent and competent

_____ Moral Booster

_____ Mentally tough

_____ Attention to details

_____ Celebrates progress

_____ Total Score

Leadership Performance Score:

200	Wow. You are perfect!
181 – 199	You are going to make a huge impact!
160 – 180	You are a good leader!
140 – 159	Keep it up. You'll make an impact.
120 – 139	You have potential to make a difference.
100 – 119	Let someone else take over for you.
Below 100	Work on being a committed follower for a while.

If you are in a leadership position, how do your teammates perceive you as a leader? How they perceive you is more important than how you perceive yourself. You just evaluated yourself on 40 different characteristics of leadership. This may have been relatively easy. Now, take the same test only thinking about how your teammates view you.

How would they score you on each of the characteristics? Be as honest as you can with yourself. Good luck!

_____ Chemically-free	_____ Mature
_____ Focused	_____ Respected and trusted
_____ Motivated	_____ Patient
_____ Good Sportsmanship	_____ Selfless
_____ Courageous	_____ Friendly and caring
_____ Humble	_____ Determined
_____ Confident but not arrogant	_____ Disciplined
_____ Good role model	_____ Positive attitude
_____ Takes initiative	_____ Charismatic
_____ Committed to team	_____ SERVE others
_____ Cooperative	_____ Innovative ideas
_____ Visionary	_____ Responsible
_____ Supportive and encouraging	_____ Goal-Oriented
_____ High level of integrity	_____ Hard Worker
_____ Accountable	_____ Forgiving
_____ Lead by example	_____ Consistent and competent
_____ Organized	_____ Moral Booster
_____ Strong communication skills	_____ Mentally tough
_____ Passionate and enthusiastic	_____ Attention to details
_____ Sense of humor	_____ Celebrates progress

_____ Total Score

Leadership Performance Score:

200	Wow. You are perfect!
181 – 199	You are going to make a huge impact!
160 – 180	You are a good leader!
140 – 159	Keep it up. You'll make an impact.
120 – 139	You have potential to make a difference.
100 – 119	Let someone else take over for you.
Below 100	Work on being a committed follower for a while.

How does your score compare with the score you received when you evaluated yourself? If your scores were similar, you may have a good sense of how you are performing as a leader. If you felt your teammates would score you higher than you did yourself, it could be a good sign that you are your own greatest critic. Just don't be too hard on yourself. It is difficult to follow someone who is constantly doubting themselves and isn't a confident leader. If you scored yourself much higher than your teammates, there should be some concern. In Chapter Five, we talked about cognitive dissonance. If applied to leadership, it would be the gap between our perceived reality of leadership, and other's perception of us.

We need to look closely at the scores and make the necessary adjustments as a leader. For example, if you gave yourself a "4" for positive attitude, committed to team, and work ethic and felt your teammates would give you a "2", and you may want to look at how you can step it up in that particular area. Otherwise, be a leader and GO MAKE A DIFFERENCE!!

APPENDIX

CHAPTER

REVIEW

QUESTIONS

* It may have been obvious that Rick believes choices are so powerful. Why?

* What has shaped your opinion about chemical use and the choices you are making in your life?

* What are the characteristics of a great leader? Does your program have someone who is that person?

* In what areas do leaders most often struggle? Any suggestions for them?

* Of the 18 recommendations given, what three apply most to you?

* What is your plan for success with those three areas?

REFERENCES
AND RESOURCES

Tavern Puzzle Collection
Tucker-Jones House, Inc
1 Enterprise Dr. East Setauket, NY 11733
(631) 642-9092
info@TavernPuzzle.com
www.TavernPuzzle.com

Denson, A. (1990), *It's One Thing to Say it*. On *Be The One*, Benson
Recording, Inc.

Kraft, D. (April, 1992) *Scoring Big*. Volleyball Monthly Magazine
91-93

FACE (Facing Alcohol Concerns through Education) The Prevention
Resource Group. www.faceproject.org

ABOUT THE AUTHOR

Over the years, people have been curious about how I started playing whole volleyball teams by myself. In the summer of 1982, I ran a Strength & Conditioning/Volleyball Camp at St. Cloud State University. At the end of the camp, I hosted a barbeque for all the high school athletes. A bunch of the guys were trash talking saying they could beat the SCSU Men's Volleyball Club Team. I was coaching and playing on the club team at that time. I eventually had enough of their "talk" and challenged them to a game by myself. They thought the idea was hilarious. We ended up playing on a bet for free meals and they lost 15-1, 15-0. That was the beginning of the "One Man Volleyball Team." I spent over 20 years traveling around the country using volleyball as a platform to share a drug-free motivational message.

Long hours of training taught me a great deal about motivation, discipline, and making the most of my abilities. Playing volleyball in high-pressure situations against some talented volleyball teams was hands on learning about the mental toughness often overlooked in the realm of performance. It was priceless from an educational standpoint; one that I could have never experienced through a book or in a classroom.

My wife Penny and I have four daughters: Gia, Sierra, Kimmy, and Hope and one son Ty. They are incredible kids. I had been coaching 16 years when Ty was born. When he was a week old, he contracted bacterial meningitis. We were told that he would never be able to see, hear, walk or talk. At that point, I resigned from coaching since we were in for a long haul with extensive therapy. My desire was to come back to coaching, but I'm grateful for how things worked out.

A few years after moving to our home in the country, I was behind our garage admiring the straight white pines on our property. I vividly remember thinking, "Hey, We could build a challenge course right here!" I could envision the details. I took on the project one day at a time and spent nearly a year studying experiential learning and the guidelines and standards of the ACCT (Association of Challenge Course Technology) for building a challenge course. With each step, I got more excited. We built a 60 foot four-sided climbing tower, a 400 foot zip line, and six other high elements ranging from 20-35 feet up in the trees. From the summer of 2002 through the summer of 2008, we had hundreds of teams visit for training and many lives were challenged and changed.

The challenge course created some great memories for my family as well with each one of our kids involved as staff. However, many coaches felt that their athletes were challenged more through the activities I could do at their facilities.   Each year I feel honored to have the opportunity to work with more than 200 athletic teams from the middle school level to national champions at the college level. I take a great deal of pride in developing training agendas picking from over 150 different challenges. The job has definitely become more of a mission than work.

My life experiences have shaped the direction and challenges of this book. From growing up on a farm and learning an incredible work ethic from my parents to teaching elementary physical education for 25 years. Many coaches and athletes have suggested that I write a book. I'm thankful for their encouraging nudges. I hope this book will help you challenge your limits, one step at a time, celebrating progress as you strive to achieve your dreams. You can't achieve tomorrow without achieving today!

Rick Rassier
3333 Division St. Suite 205
St. Cloud, MN 56301
(320) 203-7854
jump@cloudnet.com
www.rickrassier.weebly.com

Made in the USA
Charleston, SC
11 March 2014